Quick & Easy
Chicken Dishes

p

Contents

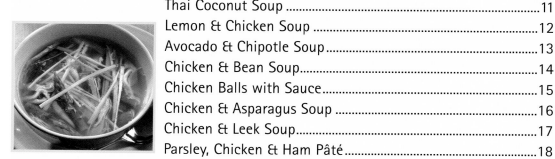

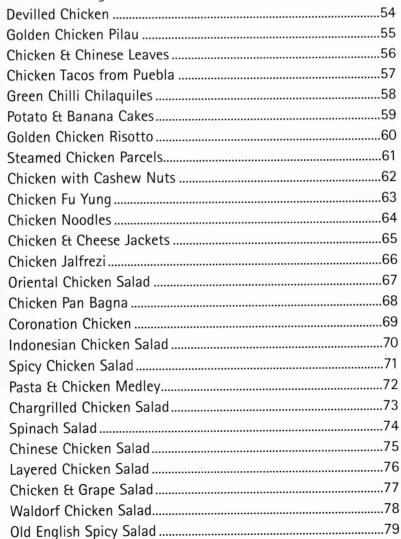

Introduction

Chicken has become justly popular around the world and plays an important part in the modern diet, being reasonably priced and nutritionally sound. A versatile meat, it lends itself to an enormous range of cooking methods and cuisines. Its unassertive flavour means that it is equally suited to cooking with both sweet and savoury flavours. Because it has a low fat content, especially without the skin, it is an ideal meat for low cholesterol and calorie-controlled diets. An excellent source of protein, chicken also contains valuable minerals, such as potassium and phosphorus, and some of the B vitamins.

Cooking Methods for Chicken

Roasting Remove any fat from the body cavity. Rinse the bird inside and out with water, then pat dry with kitchen paper. Season the cavity generously with salt and pepper and add any stuffing or herbs. Spread the breast with softened butter or oil. Set on a rack in a roasting tin or a shallow baking dish. Roast, basting two or three times with the tin juices during roasting. If the chicken is browning too quickly, cover it with foil. Test that it is done as described in Food Safety & Tips, opposite. Put the bird on a carving board and leave it to rest for at least 15 minutes before serving. Make a sauce or gravy from the juices left in the roasting tin.

Grilling A grill's intense heat quickly seals the succulent flesh beneath a crisp exterior. Place the chicken 10–15 cm/4–6 inches from a moderate heat source. If it browns too quickly, reduce the heat slightly. If chicken is grilled too near to the heat at too high a temperature, the outside will burn before the inside is cooked. If it is cooked for too long under a low heat, it will dry out. Divide the chicken into joints to ensure even cooking. Breast meat, if cooked in one piece, can be dry, so it is best cut it into chunks. Wings are best for fast grilling.

Frying This is suitable for small drumsticks, thighs and joints. Dry the chicken pieces with kitchen paper to prevent spitting and so that they brown properly. The chicken may be coated in seasoned flour, egg and breadcrumbs, or a batter. Heat a little oil

or a mixture of oil and butter in a heavy frying pan. When the oil is very hot, add the chicken pieces, skin-side down. Fry until golden brown all over, turning frequently. Drain on kitchen paper before serving.

Sautéeing This is ideal for small pieces or small birds such as poussins. Heat a little oil or a mixture of oil and butter in a heavy frying pan. Add the chicken and fry over a moderate heat until golden brown, turning frequently. Add stock or other liquid, bring to the boil, then cover and reduce the heat. Cook gently until the chicken is cooked through.

Stir-frying Skinless, boneless chicken is cut into small pieces of equal size to ensure that the meat cooks evenly and stays succulent. Preheat a wok or saucepan before adding a small amount of oil. When the oil starts to smoke, add the chicken and stir-fry with your chosen flavourings for 3–4 minutes, or until cooked through. Other ingredients can be cooked at the same time, or the chicken can be cooked by itself, then removed from the pan while you stir-fry the remaining ingredients. Return the chicken to the pan once the other ingredients are cooked.

Casseroling This is good for cooking joints from larger, more mature chickens, although smaller chickens can be cooked whole. The slow cooking produces tender meat with a good flavour. Brown the chicken in butter or oil,

or a mixture of both. Add stock, wine, or a mixture of both with seasonings and herbs, then cover and cook on top of the stove or in the oven until the chicken is tender. Add a selection of lightly sautéed vegetables about halfway through the cooking time.

Braising This method does not require liquid. Chicken pieces or a small whole chicken with vegetables are cooked slowly in a low oven. Heat oil in an ovenproof flameproof casserole and gently fry the chicken until golden. Remove it and fry the vegetables until they are almost tender. Replace the chicken, cover tightly, and cook very gently on the top of the stove or in a low oven until the chicken and vegetables are tender.

Poaching This gentle method produces tender chicken and a stock. Put a whole chicken, a bouquet garni, a leek, a carrot and an onion in a large flameproof casserole. Cover with water, season, and bring to the boil. Cover and simmer for 1½–2 hours, or until the chicken is tender. Lift it out, discard the bouquet garni. Use the stock as a sauce, and blend the vegetables to thicken the stock, or serve them with the chicken.

Food Safety & Tips

Chicken is liable to be contaminated by salmonella bacteria, which can cause severe food poisoning. When storing, handling and preparing poultry, it is vital to observe the following precautions to prevent illness:
1. Check the 'sell-by' date and the 'best before' date. After buying, take the chicken home quickly, preferably in a freezer bag or a cool box.
2. Place birds bought frozen in the freezer immediately.
3. To store in the refrigerator, remove wrappings and store giblets separately. Place the chicken in a shallow dish to catch drips. Cover loosely with foil and store on the bottom shelf for no more than two or three days depending on the 'best before' date. Avoid contact between raw chicken and cooked food during storage and preparation. Wash your hands thoroughly after handling raw chicken.
4. Prepare raw chicken on a chopping board that can be easily cleaned, such as a non-porous, plastic one.

5. Frozen birds should be defrosted before cooking. If time permits, defrost in the refrigerator for about 36 hours, or thaw for about 12 hours in a cool place. The flesh should feel soft and flexible, with no ice crystals. Bacteria breed in chicken thawing to room temperature. Cooking at high temperatures kills them, so cook the chicken as soon as possible after thawing.
6. Test that chicken is cooked thoroughly by using a meat thermometer. The thigh should reach at least 79°C/175°F when cooked. Alternatively, pierce the thickest part of a thigh with a skewer - the juices should run clear, not pink or red. Never partially cook chicken with the intention of completing cooking later.

Chicken Stock

A well-flavoured chicken stock is made from a whole bird or the wings, breast and legs. A stock made from just chicken bones and carcass cooked with vegetables and flavourings will be less rich. A simple stock can be made from giblets (not the liver, which is bitter) with carrot, onion, a bouquet garni and some peppercorns. Home-made stock can be stored in the freezer for up to six months.

To make chicken stock: place a whole chicken or wings and carcass into a large stockpot with two quartered onions. Cook until chicken and onion are evenly browned. Cover with cold water, bring to the boil, and skim off any scum from the surface. Add two chopped carrots, two chopped celery stalks, a small bunch of parsley, a few bay leaves, a thyme sprig, and a few peppercorns. Partially cover and simmer for about 3 hours. Strain into a bowl, leave to cool, then chill. Remove the fat that will have set on the surface.

KEY
Simplicity level 1 – 3 (1 easiest, 3 slightly harder)
Preparation time
Cooking time

Cream of Chicken Soup

Tarragon adds a delicate aniseed flavour to this tasty soup. If you cannot find tarragon, use parsley for a fresh taste.

NUTRITIONAL INFORMATION

Calories	420	Sugars	.........4g
Protein	........24g	Fat	..........33g
Carbohydrate	....6g	Saturates	......20g

10 mins   25 mins

SERVES 4

INGREDIENTS

4 tbsp unsalted butter

1 large onion, chopped

300 g/10½ oz cooked chicken, shredded finely

600 ml/1 pint chicken stock

1 tbsp chopped fresh tarragon

150 ml/5 fl oz double cream

salt and pepper

fresh tarragon leaves, to garnish

deep-fried croûtons, to serve

VARIATION

If you cannot find fresh tarragon, freeze-dried tarragon makes a good substitute. Single cream can be used instead of the double cream to reduce the calorie content.

1 Melt the butter in a large saucepan and fry the onion for 3 minutes.

2 Add the finely shredded chicken to the saucepan together with 300 ml/ 10 fl oz of the chicken stock. Mix the ingredients together in the pan.

3 Bring to the boil and simmer for 20 minutes. Allow to cool, then blend the soup using a liquidizer.

4 Add the remainder of the stock and season with salt and pepper.

5 Add the chopped tarragon, pour the soup into a tureen or individual serving bowls and add a swirl of cream.

6 Garnish the soup with fresh tarragon and serve with deep-fried croûtons.

Tom's Chicken Soup

The potato has been part of the Irish diet for centuries. This recipe came originally from Moira, County Down, Northern Ireland.

NUTRITIONAL INFORMATION

Calories 97	Sugars 1.8g
Protein 7.3g	Fat 2g
Carbohydrate ...4.2g	Saturates 3.3g

10 mins   1 hr 15 mins

SERVES 4

I N G R E D I E N T S

3 smoked, streaky, rindless bacon slices, chopped

500 g/1 lb 2 oz boneless chicken, chopped

2 tbsp butter

3 potatoes, chopped

3 onions, chopped

600 ml/1 pint giblet or chicken stock

600 ml/1 pint milk

salt and pepper

150 ml/5 fl oz double cream

2 tbsp chopped fresh parsley

soda bread, to serve

1 Fry the bacon and chicken gently in a large saucepan for 10 minutes.

2 Add the butter, potatoes and onions and cook for 15 minutes, stirring all the time.

3 Add the stock and milk, then bring to the boil and simmer for 45 minutes. Season with salt and pepper to taste.

4 Blend in the cream and simmer for 5 minutes. Stir in the chopped fresh parsley, then transfer the soup to a warm tureen or individual bowls and serve with Irish soda bread.

VARIATION
For a more filling, main course soup, you can add any number of different vegetables, for example leeks, celeriac or sweetcorn.

Vegetable & Chickpea Soup

A tasty soup, full of vegetables, chicken and chickpeas, with just a hint of spiciness, to serve on any occasion.

NUTRITIONAL INFORMATION

Calories 271   Sugar 6g
Protein . . . . .17g   Fats 13g
Carbohydrates . . .24g   Saturates 2g

 10 mins   55 mins

SERVES 4–6

I N G R E D I E N T S

3 tbsp olive oil

1 large onion, finely chopped

2–3 garlic cloves, crushed

½–1 red chilli, deseeded and very finely chopped

1 skinless, boneless chicken breast (about 150 g/5½ oz), sliced thickly

2 celery sticks, chopped finely

175 g/6 oz carrots, grated coarsely

1.3 litres/2¼ pints chicken stock

2 bay leaves

½ tsp dried oregano

¼ tsp ground cinnamon

400 g/14 oz can of chickpeas, drained

2 tomatoes, peeled, deseeded and chopped

1 tbsp tomato purée

salt and pepper

chopped fresh coriander or parsley, to garnish

corn or wheat tortillas, to serve

1 Heat the oil in a large saucepan and fry the onion, garlic and chilli very gently until they are softened but not coloured.

2 Add the chicken to the saucepan and continue to cook until well sealed and lightly browned.

3 Add the celery, carrots, stock, bay leaves, oregano, cinnamon, and salt and pepper. Bring to the boil, then cover and simmer gently for about 20 minutes, or until the chicken is tender and cooked throughout.

4 Remove the chicken from the soup and chop it finely, or cut it into narrow strips.

5 Return the chicken to the pan with the chickpeas, tomatoes and tomato purée. Simmer, covered, for a further 15–20 minutes. Discard the bay leaves, then adjust the seasoning.

6 Serve very hot sprinkled with coriander or parsley and accompanied by warmed tortillas.

Chicken Consommé

This is a very flavourful soup, especially if you make it from real chicken stock. Egg shells are used to give a crystal clear appearance.

NUTRITIONAL INFORMATION

Calories	96	Sugars 1g
Protein	........11g	Fat 1g
Carbohydrate	....1g	Saturates 0.4g

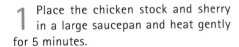

10 mins   55 mins

SERVES 4

I N G R E D I E N T S

1.7 litres/3 pints chicken stock

150 ml/5 fl oz medium sherry

4 egg whites, plus egg shells

125 g/4¼ oz cooked lean chicken, sliced thinly

salt and pepper

1 Place the chicken stock and sherry in a large saucepan and heat gently for 5 minutes.

2 Add the egg whites and the egg shells to the chicken stock and whisk until the mixture begins to boil. When the mixture boils, remove the pan from the heat and allow the mixture to subside for 10 minutes. Repeat this process three times. This allows the egg white to trap the sediments in the chicken stock to clarify the soup.

3 Let the chicken consommé cool for 5 minutes.

4 Carefully place a piece of fine muslin over a clean saucepan. Ladle the soup over the muslin and strain the liquid into the saucepan.

5 Repeat this process twice, then gently reheat the consommé. Season with salt and pepper to taste, add the chicken slices to the consommé and serve immediately.

COOK'S TIP

For extra colour, add a garnish to the soup. Use a tablespoon each of finely diced carrot, celery and turnip or some finely chopped herbs, such as parsley or tarragon.

Chicken & Rice Soup

This soup is a good way of using up leftover cooked chicken and rice. Any kind of rice is suitable, from white or brown long-grain rice to wild rice.

NUTRITIONAL INFORMATION

Calories 165	Sugars 3g	
Protein 14g	Fat 4g	
Carbohydrate ...19g	Saturates 1g	

5 mins, plus
20 mins for rice

30 mins

SERVES 4

I N G R E D I E N T S

1.5 litres/2¾ pints chicken stock
(see Cook's Tip)

2 small carrots, very thinly sliced

1 stalk celery, finely diced

1 baby leek, halved lengthways and
thinly sliced

115 g/4 oz tiny peas, defrosted if frozen

175 g/6 oz cooked rice

150 g/5½ oz cooked chicken, sliced

2 tsp chopped fresh tarragon

1 tbsp chopped fresh parsley

salt and pepper

fresh parsley sprigs, to garnish

1 Put the stock in a large saucepan and add the carrots, celery and leek. Bring to the boil, reduce the heat to low and simmer gently, partially covered, for 10 minutes.

2 Stir in the peas, rice and chicken and continue cooking for a further 10–15 minutes, or until the vegetables are tender.

3 Add the chopped tarragon and parsley, then taste and adjust the seasoning, adding salt and pepper as needed.

4 Ladle the soup into warm bowls, garnish with parsley and serve.

COOK'S TIP

If the stock you are using is a little on the weak side, or if you have used a stock cube, add the herbs at the beginning, so that they can flavour the stock for a longer time.

Thai Coconut Soup

This soup makes a change from traditional chicken soup. It is spicy, and garnished with a generous quantity of fresh coriander leaves.

NUTRITIONAL INFORMATION

Calories	76	Sugars	........2g
Protein	........13g	Fat	..........1g
Carbohydrate	....3g	Saturates	.......0g

 5 mins   40 mins

SERVES 4

INGREDIENTS

1.2 litres/2 pints chicken stock

200 g/7 oz skinless boned chicken

1 fresh chilli, split lengthways
    and deseeded

7.5 cm/3 inch piece lemon grass,
    split lengthways

3–4 lime leaves

2.5 cm/1 inch piece fresh ginger root,
    peeled and sliced

120 ml/4 fl oz coconut milk

6–8 spring onions, sliced diagonally

¼ tsp chilli purée, to taste

salt

fresh coriander leaves, to garnish

1 Put the stock in a pan with the chicken, chilli, lemon grass, lime leaves and ginger. Bring almost to the boil, reduce the heat, cover and simmer for 20–25 minutes, or until the chicken is cooked through and firm to the touch.

2 Remove the chicken from the pan and strain the stock. When the chicken is cool, slice thinly or shred into bite-sized pieces.

3 Return the stock to the saucepan and heat to simmering. Stir in the coconut milk and spring onions. Add the chicken and continue simmering for about 10 minutes, or until the soup is heated through and the flavours have mingled.

4 Stir in the chilli purée. Season to taste with salt and, if wished, add a little more chilli purée.

5 Ladle into warm bowls and float fresh coriander leaves on top to serve.

COOK'S TIP

Once the stock is flavoured and the chicken cooked, this soup is very quick to finish. If you wish, poach the chicken and strain the stock ahead of time. Store in the refrigerator separately.

Lemon & Chicken Soup

This delicately flavoured summer soup is surprisingly easy to make and may be prepared well in advance of its serving time.

NUTRITIONAL INFORMATION

Calories	506	Sugars	.........4g
Protein	........19g	Fat	..........31g
Carbohydrate	...41g	Saturates	......19g

 10 mins   1 hr 10 mins

SERVES 4

I N G R E D I E N T S

4 tbsp butter

8 shallots, thinly sliced

2 carrots, thinly sliced

2 celery sticks, thinly sliced

225 g/8 oz chicken breasts, finely chopped

3 lemons, thinly pared and juiced, with slices reserved for garnish

1.2 litres/2 pints chicken stock

225 g/8 oz dried spaghetti, broken into small pieces

salt and white pepper

150 ml/5 fl oz double cream

T O   G A R N I S H

fresh parsley sprig

3 lemon slices, halved

1 Melt the butter in a large saucepan. Add the shallots, carrots, celery and chicken. Cook over a low heat for 8 minutes.

2 Pare the lemons thinly, and blanch the rind in boiling water for 3 minutes. Squeeze the lemon juice keep it.

3 Add the lemon rind and juice, and the stock to the pan. Bring slowly to the boil over a low heat, and simmer, stirring occasionally, for 40 minutes,

4 Add the spaghetti to the pan and cook for 15 minutes. Season, and add the cream. Heat through, but do not allow the soup to boil or it will curdle.

5 Pour the soup into a tureen. Serve garnished with parsley and lemon.

COOK'S TIP

You can prepare this soup up to the end of Step 3 in advance, so that all you need do before serving is heat it through before adding the pasta and the finishing touches.

Avocado & Chipotle Soup

This soup evolved from the street food stalls of Mexico City. Rich avocado, shreds of chicken and the smoky hit of chipotle make it special.

NUTRITIONAL INFORMATION

Calories	218	Sugars	.........1g
Protein	........28g	Fat	...........11g
Carbohydrate	....2g	Saturates	.......2g

 15 mins   5 mins

SERVES 4

INGREDIENTS

1.5 litres/2¾ pints chicken stock

2–3 garlic cloves, finely chopped

1–2 chipotle chillies, cut into very thin strips (see Cook's Tip)

1 avocado, diced

lime or lemon juice, for tossing

3–5 spring onions, thinly sliced

350–400 g/12–14 oz cooked chicken breast, torn or cut into shreds or thin strips

2 tbsp chopped fresh coriander

TO SERVE

1 lime, cut into wedges

handful of tortilla chips, optional

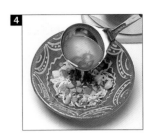

1 Place the stock in a pan with the garlic and chipotle chillies and bring to the boil.

2 Meanwhile, cut the avocado in half around the large stone. Twist apart, then remove the stone with a knife. Carefully peel off the skin, dice the flesh and toss in the citrus juice to prevent the fruit discolouring.

3 Arrange the thinly sliced spring onions, cooked chicken, diced avocado and fresh coriander equally in the bases of 4 soup bowls or in a single large serving bowl.

4 Ladle the hot stock over the arrangement, and serve with the wedges of lime and a handful of tortilla chips, if using.

COOK'S TIP
Chipotle chillies are smoked and dried jalapeño chillies, available from specialist stores. Chipotles canned in adobo marinade are best for this recipe. Drain before using. Dried chipotles need to be reconstituted for use.

Chicken & Bean Soup

This hearty and nourishing soup, combining chickpeas and chicken, is an ideal starter for a family supper, or it can make a snack on its own.

NUTRITIONAL INFORMATION

Calories	347	Sugars	.........2g
Protein	........28g	Fat	...........11g
Carbohydrate	...37g	Saturates	.......4g

15 mins   2 hrs 30 mins

SERVES 4

INGREDIENTS

2 tbsp butter

3 spring onions, chopped

2 garlic cloves, crushed

1 fresh marjoram sprig, finely chopped

350 g/12 oz boned chicken breasts, diced

1.2 litres/2 pints chicken stock

350 g/12 oz can chickpeas, drained

1 bouquet garni

1 red pepper, diced

1 green pepper, diced

115 g/4 oz small dried pasta shapes,
    such as elbow macaroni

salt and white pepper

croûtons, to serve

COOK'S TIP

To use dried chickpeas.
Cover with cold water and set aside to soak for 5–8 hours.
Drain and add the beans to the soup, according to the recipe, and allow an additional 30 minutes–1 hour cooking time.

1 Melt the butter in a large saucepan. Add the spring onions, garlic, sprig of fresh marjoram and the diced chicken and cook, stirring frequently, over a medium heat for 5 minutes.

2 Add the chicken stock, chickpeas and bouquet garni and season with salt and white pepper.

3 Bring the soup to the boil, lower the heat and simmer for about 2 hours.

4 Add the diced peppers and pasta shapes to the pan, then simmer for a further 20 minutes.

5 Transfer the soup to a warm tureen. To serve, ladle the soup into individual serving bowls and serve immediately, garnished with the croûtons.

Chicken Balls with Sauce

Serve these bite-sized chicken starters warm as a snack, with drinks, or packed cold for a picnic or a lunch box treat.

NUTRITIONAL INFORMATION

Calories 214	Sugars 29g
Protein 20g	Fat 13g
Carbohydrate 5g	Saturates 2g

10 mins   20 mins

SERVES 4

INGREDIENTS

2 large boneless, skinless chicken breasts

3 tbsp vegetable oil

2 shallots, finely chopped

½ celery stick, finely chopped

1 garlic clove, crushed

2 tbsp light soy sauce

1 small egg

salt and pepper

1 bunch spring onions

spring onion tassels, to garnish

DIPPING SAUCE

3 tbsp dark soy sauce

1 tbsp rice wine

1 tsp sesame seeds

1 Cut the chicken into 2 cm/¾ inch pieces. Heat half of the oil in a frying pan or wok and stir-fry the chicken over a high heat for 2–3 minutes, or until golden. Remove from the pan with a perforated spoon; set aside.

2 Add the shallots, celery and garlic to the pan and stir-fry for 1–2 minutes, or until softened but not browned.

3 Place the chicken, shallots, celery and garlic in a food processor and process until finely minced. Add 1 tablespoon of the light soy sauce, just enough egg to make a fairly firm mixture, and then add salt and pepper.

4 Trim the spring onions and then cut into 5 cm/2 inch lengths. Make the dipping sauce by mixing together the dark soy sauce, rice wine and sesame seeds, then set aside.

5 Shape the chicken mixture into 16–18 walnut-sized balls. Heat the remaining oil in the frying pan or wok and then stir-fry the balls in small batches for 4–5 minutes, or until they are golden brown. As each batch is cooked drain on kitchen paper and keep hot.

6 Stir-fry the spring onions for 1–2 minutes, or until they begin to soften, then stir in the remaining light soy sauce. Serve them with the hot chicken balls and a bowl of dipping sauce on a serving platter. Garnish the dish with the spring onion tassels.

Chicken & Asparagus Soup

This light, clear soup has a delicate flavour of asparagus and freshly picked herbs. Use a good quality stock for best results.

NUTRITIONAL INFORMATION

Calories 224   Sugars 2g
Protein ....27g   Fat 5g
Carbohydrate ...12g   Saturates 1g

5 mins   15 mins

SERVES 4

INGREDIENTS

225 g/8 oz fresh asparagus

850 ml/1½ pints fresh chicken stock
  (see page 5)

150 ml/5 fl oz dry white wine

1 sprig each fresh parsley, dill and tarragon

1 garlic clove

60 g/2¼ oz vermicelli rice noodles

350 g/12 oz lean cooked chicken,
  finely shredded

salt and white pepper

1 small leek, finely shredded

1 Wash the asparagus and trim away the woody ends. Cut each spear into pieces 4 cm/1½ inches long.

2 Pour the stock and wine into a large saucepan and bring to the boil.

3 Wash the herbs and tie them with clean string. Peel the garlic clove and add, with the herbs, to the saucepan together with the asparagus and noodles. Cover and simmer for 5 minutes.

4 Stir in the chicken and plenty of seasoning. Simmer gently for a further 3-4 minutes, or until heated through.

5 Trim the leek, slice it down the centre and wash under running water to remove any dirt. Shake dry and shred finely.

6 Remove the herbs and garlic from the pan and discard. Ladle the soup into warm bowls, sprinkle with shredded leek and serve at once.

VARIATION

You can use any of your favourite herbs in this recipe, but choose those with a subtle flavour so that they do not overpower the asparagus. Small, tender asparagus spears give the best results and flavour.

Chicken & Leek Soup

This satisfying soup may be served as a main course. Add rice and peppers to make it still more hearty, and colourful.

NUTRITIONAL INFORMATION

Calories 183   Sugar 4g
Protein . . . . .21g   Fats 9g
Carbohydrates . . . .4g   Saturates 5g

 5 mins   🕐 1¼ hrs, plus 20 mins for rice

SERVES 4–6

INGREDIENTS

2 tbsp butter

350 g/12 oz leeks

350 g/12 oz boneless chicken

1.2 litres/2 pints fresh chicken stock (see page 5)

1 bouquet garni sachet

8 stoned prunes, halved

salt and white pepper

115 g/4 oz cooked rice and diced peppers, optional

1. Melt the butter in a large saucepan. Cut the leeks into 2.5 cm/1 inch pieces.

2. Add the chicken and leeks to the saucepan and fry for 8 minutes.

3. Next add the chicken stock and bouquet garni sachet and stir together well.

4. Season the mixture well with salt and freshly ground pepper to taste.

5. Bring the Chicken and Leek Soup to the boil and simmer for 45 minutes.

6. Add the stoned prunes to the saucepan with the cooked rice and diced peppers, if using, and simmer for about 20 minutes.

7. Remove the bouquet garni sachet from the soup and discard. Serve the soup immediately.

VARIATION

Instead of the bouquet garni sachet, you can use a bunch of fresh mixed herbs, tied together with string. Choose herbs such as parsley, thyme and rosemary.

Parsley, Chicken & Ham Pâté

Pâté is easy to make at home, and this combination of lean chicken and ham mixed with herbs is especially straightforward.

NUTRITIONAL INFORMATION

Calories 119	Sugars 2g
Protein 20g	Fat 3g
Carbohydrate 2g	Saturates 1g

 10 mins   30 mins to chill

SERVES 4

INGREDIENTS

225 g/8 oz lean, cooked skinless chicken

100 g/3½ oz lean ham, trimmed

small bunch fresh parsley

1 tsp lime rind, grated

2 tbsp lime juice

1 garlic clove, peeled

125 ml/4 fl oz low-fat natural fromage frais

salt and pepper

1 tsp lime rind, to garnish

TO SERVE

lime wedges

crisp bread

green salad

1 Dice the chicken and ham and place in a blender or food processor.

2 Add the parsley, lime rind and lime juice, and garlic to the chicken and ham, and process well until finely minced. Alternatively, chop the chicken, ham, parsley and garlic finely, and place them in a bowl. Mix gently with the lime rind and juice.

3 Transfer the mixture to a bowl and mix in the low-fat fromage frais. Season with salt and pepper to taste, cover and leave to chill in the refrigerator for about 30 minutes.

4 Pile the pâté into individual serving dishes and garnish with lime rind. Serve the pâtés with lime wedges, crisp bread and a fresh green salad.

VARIATION

This pâté can be made successfully with other kinds of minced, lean, cooked meat such as turkey, beef and pork. Alternatively, replace the meat with peeled prawns and/or white crab meat, or with canned tuna in brine, drained.

Sticky Ginger Chicken Wings

A finger-licking starter of chicken wings or drumsticks which is ideal for parties (have finger bowls ready).

NUTRITIONAL INFORMATION

Calories 416   Sugars 5g
Protein . . . . .41g   Fat 25g
Carbohydrate . . . .7g   Saturates 7g

 15 mins, plus several hrs for marinating   15 mins

SERVES 4

I N G R E D I E N T S

2 garlic cloves, peeled

1 piece stem ginger in syrup

1 tsp coriander seeds

2 tbsp stem ginger syrup

2 tbsp dark soy sauce

1 tbsp lime juice

1 tsp sesame oil

12 chicken wings

lime wedges and fresh coriander leaves, to garnish

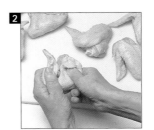

1 Chop the garlic and ginger roughly. In a pestle and mortar, crush the garlic, stem ginger and coriander seeds to a paste, gradually working in the ginger syrup, soy sauce, lime juice and sesame oil.

2 Tuck the pointed tip of each chicken wing underneath the thicker end of the wing to make a neat triangular shape. Place in a large bowl.

3 Add the garlic and ginger paste to the bowl and toss the chicken wings in the mixture to coat evenly. Cover and leave in the refrigerator to marinate for several hours or overnight.

4 Arrange the chicken wings in one layer on a foil-lined grill pan, then grill under a medium-hot grill for 12–15 minutes, turning them occasionally, until golden brown and thoroughly cooked.

5 Alternatively, cook on a lightly oiled barbecue grill over medium-hot coals for 12–15 minutes. To serve, garnish with lime wedges and fresh coriander.

COOK'S TIP

To test if the chicken is cooked, pierce it deeply through the thickest part of the flesh. When it is cooked, the chicken juices are clear, with no trace of pink. If there is any trace of pink, cook for a few more minutes.

Lemon Grass Skewers

An unusual recipe in which fresh lemon grass stalks are used as skewers. They impart their delicate lemon flavour to the chicken mixture.

NUTRITIONAL INFORMATION

Calories	140	Sugars	.........2g
Protein	........19g	Fat	...........7g
Carbohydrate	....2g	Saturates	.......1g

 10 mins   20 mins

SERVES 4

I N G R E D I E N T S

2 long or 4 short lemon grass stalks

2 large boneless, skinless chicken breasts (about 400 g/14 oz), roughly chopped

1 small egg white

1 carrot, finely grated

1 small red chilli, deseeded and chopped

2 tbsp fresh garlic chives, chopped

2 tbsp fresh coriander, chopped

salt and pepper

1 tbsp sunflower oil

coriander and lime slices, to garnish

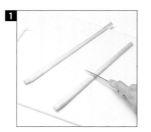

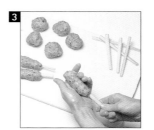

1 If the lemon grass stalks are long, cut them in half across the middle to make 4 short lengths. Cut each stalk in half lengthways, so you have 8 lemon grass sticks altogether.

COOK'S TIP

If you can't find whole lemon grass stalks, use wooden or bamboo skewers instead, and add ½ teaspoon ground lemon grass to the mixture with the other flavourings.

2 Place the the chicken pieces in a food processor with the egg white. Process to a smooth paste, then add the carrot, chilli, chives, coriander and salt and pepper. Process for a few seconds to mix well.

3 Chill the mixture in the refrigerator for about 15 minutes. Divide the mixture into 8 equal portions, and use your hands to shape the mixture around the lemon grass 'skewers'.

4 Brush the skewers with oil and grill under a preheated medium-hot grill for 4–6 minutes, turning them occasionally, until golden brown and thoroughly cooked. Alternatively, barbecue over medium-hot coals.

5 Serve hot, and garnish with slices of lime and coriander.

Chicken Scallops

Served in scallop shells, this unusual chicken dish makes a stylish presentation for a starter or a light lunch.

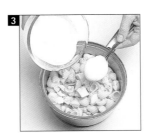
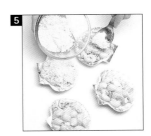

NUTRITIONAL INFORMATION

Calories	532	Sugars	.........3g
Protein	........25g	Fat	.........34g
Carbohydrate	...33g	Saturates	......14g

10 mins   35 mins

SERVES 4

INGREDIENTS

175 g/6 oz short-cut macaroni, or other short pasta shapes

3 tbsp vegetable oil, plus extra for brushing

1 onion, chopped finely

3 rashers unsmoked collar or back bacon, rind removed, chopped

125 g/4¼ oz button mushrooms, sliced thinly or chopped

175 g/6 oz cooked chicken, diced

175 ml/6 fl oz crème fraîche

4 tbsp dry breadcrumbs

60 g/2¼ oz mature Cheddar, grated

salt and pepper

flat-leaved parsley sprigs, to garnish

1 Cook the pasta in a large pan of boiling salted water with 1 tablespoon of oil for 8–10 minutes. Drain the pasta, return to the pan and cover.

2 Heat the grill to medium. Heat the remaining oil in a pan over medium heat and fry the onion until translucent. Add the bacon and mushrooms and cook for 3–4 minutes, stirring once or twice.

3 Stir in the pasta, chicken and crème fraîche and season to taste with salt and pepper.

4 Brush four large scallop shells with oil. Spoon in the chicken mixture and smooth to make neat mounds.

5 Mix together the breadcrumbs and cheese, and sprinkle over the top of the shells. Press the topping lightly into the chicken mixture, and grill for 4–5 minutes, until golden brown and bubbling. Garnish with sprigs of flat-leaved parsley, and serve hot.

Chicken & Mango Stir-Fry

A colourful mix of exotic flavours works surprisingly well in a dish that is easy and quick to cook – ideal for a mid-week family meal.

NUTRITIONAL INFORMATION

Calories	200	Sugars	.........5g
Protein	........23g	Fat	...........6g
Carbohydrate	....7g	Saturates	.......1g

 15 mins   12 mins

SERVES 4

I N G R E D I E N T S

6 boneless, skinless chicken thighs

2 tsp fresh root ginger, grated

1 garlic clove, crushed

1 small red chilli, deseeded

1 large red pepper

4 spring onions

200 g/7 oz mangetouts

100 g/3½ oz baby corn cobs

1 large, firm, ripe mango

2 tbsp sunflower oil

1 tbsp light soy sauce

3 tbsp rice wine or sherry

1 tsp sesame oil

salt and pepper

snipped chives, to garnish

1 Cut the chicken into long, thin strips and place in a bowl. Mix together the ginger, garlic and chilli, then stir in to the chicken strips to coat them evenly.

2 Slice the pepper thinly, cutting diagonally. Trim and diagonally slice the spring onions. Cut the mangetouts and corn in half diagonally. Peel the mango, remove the stone and slice thinly.

3 Heat the oil in a large frying pan or wok over a high heat. Add the chicken and stir-fry for 4–5 minutes, or until just turning golden brown. Add the peppers and stir-fry over a medium heat for 4–5 minutes to soften them.

4 Add the spring onions, mangetouts and the corn and stir-fry for a further minute.

5 Mix together the soy sauce, rice wine or sherry and sesame oil in a separate bowl and stir the mixture into the wok with the rest of the ingredients. Add the mango and stir gently for 1 minute to heat thoroughly.

6 Adjust the seasoning with salt and pepper to taste and serve immediately. Garnish with chives.

Green Chicken Curry

Thai curries are traditionally very hot, and they make a little go a long way.
The spiced juices are eaten with rice to 'stretch' a small amount of meat.

NUTRITIONAL INFORMATION

Calories	193	Sugars	.........9g
Protein	.......22g	Fat	..........8g
Carbohydrate	....9g	Saturates	.......1g

 5 mins　　 45 mins

SERVES 4

I N G R E D I E N T S

6 boneless, skinless chicken thighs

400 ml/14 fl oz coconut milk

2 garlic cloves, crushed

2 tbsp Thai fish sauce

2 tbsp Thai green curry paste

12 baby aubergines (or Thai pea aubergines)

3 green chillies, finely chopped

3 kaffir lime leaves, shredded

4 tbsp fresh coriander, chopped

salt and pepper

boiled rice, to serve

1 Cut the chicken into bite-sized pieces. Pour the coconut milk into a large pan or a wok over a high heat and bring to the boil.

2 Add the chicken, garlic and fish sauce to the pan and bring back to the boil. Lower the heat and simmer gently for 30 minutes, or until the chicken is tender.

3 Remove the chicken from the mixture with a perforated spoon. Set aside and keep warm.

4 Stir the green curry paste into the pan, add the aubergines, chillies and lime leaves and then simmer for 5 minutes.

5 Return the chicken to the pan and bring to the boil. Adjust the seasoning to taste with salt and pepper, then stir in the coriander. Serve the Green Chicken Curry with boiled rice.

COOK'S TIP
Baby aubergines, or 'pea aubergines' as they are called in Thailand, are traditionally used, but not always available outside the country. If you can't find them in an Oriental food shop, use chopped ordinary aubergine or a few green peas.

Spicy Garlic Chicken

The intense flavours of this dish are brought out by gentle cooking. The meat should seem almost to fall off the bone and melt into the sauce.

NUTRITIONAL INFORMATION

Calories 282   Sugars 3g
Protein . . . . .29g   Fat 16g
Carbohydrate . . . .5g   Saturates 3g

 10 mins   50 mins

SERVES 4

INGREDIENTS

4 garlic cloves, chopped

4 shallots, chopped

2 small red chillies, deseeded and chopped

1 lemon grass stalk, finely chopped

1 tbsp fresh coriander, chopped

1 tsp shrimp paste

½ tsp ground cinnamon

1 tbsp tamarind paste

2 tbsp vegetable oil

8 small chicken joints, such as drumsticks or thighs

300 ml/10 fl oz chicken stock

1 tbsp Thai fish sauce

1 tbsp smooth peanut butter

salt and pepper

4 tbsp toasted peanuts, chopped

stir-fried vegetables and boiled noodles, to serve

1 Place the garlic, shallots, chillies, lemon grass, coriander and shrimp paste in a pestle and mortar and grind to an almost smooth paste. Add the cinnamon and tamarind paste to the mixture.

2 Heat the oil in a wok or a wide frying pan. Add the chicken joints, turning often, until they are golden brown on all sides. Remove them from the wok and keep hot. Tip away any excess fat.

3 Add the spice paste to the wok or pan and stir over a medium heat until lightly browned. Stir in the stock and return the chicken to the pan.

4 Bring to the boil, then cover tightly, lower the heat and simmer for 25–30 minutes, stirring occasionally, until the chicken is tender and thoroughly cooked. Stir in the fish sauce and peanut butter and simmer the mixture gently for a further 10 minutes.

5 Adjust the seasoning with salt and pepper to taste and scatter the toasted peanuts over the chicken. Serve hot, with colourful stir-fry vegetables and noodles.

Spanish Chicken with Garlic

Slow cooking removes any harsh flavouring from the garlic cloves and makes them perfectly tender in this simple dish.

NUTRITIONAL INFORMATION

Calories 496   Sugars 1g
Protein . . . . .41g   Fat 22g
Carbohydrate . . .15g   Saturates 5g

 10 mins   50 mins

SERVES 4

INGREDIENTS

2–3 tbsp plain flour

cayenne pepper

4 chicken quarters or other joints, patted dry

4–5 tbsp olive oil

20 large garlic cloves, halved and green cores removed

1 large bay leaf

450 ml/16 fl oz chicken stock

4 tbsp dry white wine

salt and pepper

chopped fresh parsley, to garnish

1 Put 2 tablespoons of the flour in a plastic bag and season to taste with cayenne pepper and salt and pepper. Add each chicken piece to the bag and shake until lightly coated, then shake off the excess.

2 Heat 3 tablespoons of the olive oil in a large frying pan. Add the garlic cloves and fry for about 2 minutes. Remove with a slotted spoon and set aside.

3 Add the chicken pieces to the pan, skin-side down, and fry for 5 minutes, or until the skin is golden brown. Turn and fry for a further 5 minutes, adding an extra 1–2 tablespoons oil if necessary.

4 Return the garlic to the pan. Add the bay leaf, stock and wine and bring to the boil. Lower the heat, cover, and simmer for 25 minutes, or until the chicken is tender.

5 Using a slotted spoon, transfer the chicken to a serving platter and keep warm. Bring the cooking liquid to the boil, with the garlic, and boil until reduced to about 250 ml/9 fl oz. Adjust the seasoning, if necessary.

6 Spoon the sauce over the chicken pieces and scatter the garlic cloves. Garnish with parsley and serve.

COOK'S TIP

The cooked garlic cloves are delicious mashed into a purée on the side of the plate for smearing on the chicken pieces.

Chicken Basquaise

Sweet peppers, an ingredient often used in the Basque cooking of France, are combined in this dish with the traditional air-dried ham of Bayonne.

NUTRITIONAL INFORMATION

Calories	559	Sugars	.........8g
Protein	........50g	Fat	..........21g
Carbohydrate	...44g	Saturates	.......6g

20 mins   1 hr 30 mins

SERVES 4–5

INGREDIENTS

1.3 kg/3 lb chicken, cut into 8 pieces

flour, for dusting

2–3 tbsp olive oil

1 large onion (preferably Spanish), thickly sliced

2 peppers, deseeded and cut lengthways into thick strips

2 garlic cloves

150 g/5½ oz spicy chorizo sausage, peeled, if necessary, and cut into 1 cm/½ inch pieces

1 tbsp tomato purée

200 g/7 oz long-grain white rice or medium-grain Spanish rice, such as Valencia

450 ml/16 fl oz chicken stock

1 tsp crushed dried chillies

½ tsp dried thyme

120 g/4¼ oz Bayonne or other air-dried ham, diced

12 dry-cured black olives

2 tbsp chopped fresh flat-leaved parsley

salt and pepper

1 Dry the chicken pieces well with kitchen paper. Put about 2 tablespoons flour into a plastic bag, season with salt and pepper and add the chicken pieces. Seal the bag and shake to coat the chicken.

2 Heat 2 tablespoons of the oil in a large casserole. Add the chicken and cook for 15 minutes. Transfer to a plate.

3 Heat the remaining oil in the casserole and add the onion and peppers. Reduce the heat and stir-fry briefly. Add the garlic, chorizo and tomato purée and stir for about 3 minutes. Add the rice and cook for about 2 minutes, stirring to coat.

4 Add the stock, crushed chillies and thyme and seasoning. Bring to the boil. Return the chicken to the pan, cover and cook over a low heat for about 45 minutes.

5 Gently stir the ham, black olives and half the parsley into the rice mixture. Re-cover and heat through for a further 5 minutes. Sprinkle with the remaining parsley, and serve.

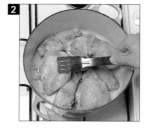
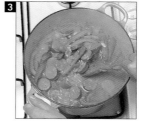

Chicken in Green Salsa

Chicken breasts bathed in a fragrant sauce make a delicate dish, perfect for dinner parties. Serve with rice to complete the meal.

NUTRITIONAL INFORMATION

Calories	349	Sugars	.........7g
Protein	........34g	Fat	..........20g
Carbohydrate	...10g	Saturates	......12g

10 mins   25 mins

SERVES 4

I N G R E D I E N T S

4 chicken breast fillets

salt and pepper

flour, for dredging

2–3 tbsp butter or combination of butter and oil

450 g/1 lb mild green salsa or puréed tomatillos

225 ml/8 fl oz chicken stock

1–2 garlic cloves, finely chopped

3–5 tbsp chopped fresh coriander

½ fresh green chilli, deseeded and chopped

½ tsp ground cumin

T O   S E R V E

225 ml/8 fl oz soured cream

several leaves cos lettuce, shredded

3–5 spring onions, thinly sliced

coarsely chopped fresh coriander

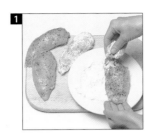  

1 Sprinkle the chicken with salt and pepper, then dredge in flour. Shake off the excess.

2 Melt the butter in a frying pan, add the chicken fillets and cook over a medium-high heat, turning once, until they are golden but not cooked through – they will continue to cook slightly in the sauce. Remove from the pan and set aside.

3 Place the salsa, chicken stock, garlic, coriander, chilli and cumin in a pan and bring to the boil. Reduce the heat to a low simmer. Add the chicken breasts to the sauce, spooning the sauce over the chicken. Continue to cook for up to 15 minutes, or until the chicken is cooked through.

4 Remove the chicken breasts from the pan and season with salt and pepper to taste. Serve with the soured cream, the shredded lettuce leaves, the sliced spring onions and the chopped fresh coriander leaves.

Citrus-marinated Chicken

This is a great dish for a summer meal. The marinade gives the chicken an appetizing flavour and helps keeps it succulent and moist during cooking.

NUTRITIONAL INFORMATION

Calories 315	Sugars 2g
Protein 42g	Fat 41g
Carbohydrate 4g	Saturates 6g

 10 mins, plus at least 1 hr to marinate   25 mins

SERVES 4

I N G R E D I E N T S

1 chicken, cut into 4 pieces

1 tbsp mild chilli powder

1 tbsp paprika

2 tsp ground cumin

1 orange, juice and rind

3 limes, juiced

pinch of sugar

8–10 garlic cloves, finely chopped

1 bunch fresh coriander, coarsely chopped

2–3 tbsp extra-virgin olive oil

50 ml/2 fl oz beer, tequila or pineapple juice, optional

salt and pepper

TO SERVE

fresh coriander sprigs

lime wedges

tomato, pepper and spring onion salad

1 Place the chicken in a non-metallic dish. To make the marinade, mix the remaining ingredients in a bowl and season.

2 Pour the marinade over the chicken, turn to coat well, then leave to marinate for at least an hour at room temperature. If possible, leave for 24 hours in the refrigerator to marinate.

3 Remove the chicken from the marinade and pat dry thoroughly with kitchen paper.

4 Put the chicken on a grill pan and place under a preheated grill for 20–25 minutes, turning once, until the chicken is cooked through. Alternatively, cook in a ridged pan. Brush with the marinade occasionally. Pierce a thick part with a skewer – the juices should run clear.

5 Garnish with coriander and serve with lime wedges and a refreshing side salad.

Poussins in Green Marinade

Steeped before cooking in a green herb marinade, these elegant poussins are packed with lively Mexican flavours.

NUTRITIONAL INFORMATION

Calories 614	Sugars 6g
Protein 44g	Fat 49g
Carbohydrate 8g	Saturates 19g

10 mins, plus at least 3 hrs to marinate   45 mins

SERVES 4

I N G R E D I E N T S

10 garlic cloves, chopped

1 lime, juiced

1 bunch fresh coriander, finely chopped

½ fresh green chilli, deseeded and chopped

1 tsp ground cumin

4 poussins

350 g/12 oz crème fraîche

1 red pepper, roasted, peeled, deseeded and diced

¼–1 tsp marinade from chipotle canned in adobo, or chipotle salsa

3–5 spring onions, thinly sliced

handful of toasted pumpkin seeds

salt and pepper

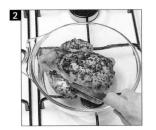

1 Combine 9 garlic cloves with the lime juice, three-quarters of the fresh coriander, the chilli and half the cumin in a bowl. Press the mixture onto the poussins and marinate for at least 3 hours in the refrigerator, or preferably overnight.

2 Place the poussins in a roasting tin and cook in a preheated oven at 200°C/400°F/Gas Mark 6. After 15 minutes remove from the oven and check whether they are cooked, by piercing the thigh with a knife. If the juices do not run clear, return to the oven and continue to roast.

3 Meanwhile, mix the crème fraîche with the pepper, chipotle marinade and the remaining garlic and cumin. Season with salt and pepper to taste.

4 Serve each poussin individually with a spoonful of the pepper sauce and a sprinkling of the remaining fresh coriander, the spring onions and the pumpkin seeds. Serve right away while still piping hot.

VARIATION

For barbecued lamb, skewer lamb chunks, such as shoulder or leg, onto metal or soaked bamboo skewers. Marinate in the green herbed marinade as in Step 1, then cook over the hot coals of a barbecue.

Chicken & Potato Casserole

Small new potatoes are ideal for this recipe because they can be cooked whole. Cut larger potatoes in half or into chunks before using them.

NUTRITIONAL INFORMATION

Calories	856	Sugars	....7g
Protein	....35g	Fat	....58g
Carbohydrate	...40g	Saturates	....26g

 15 mins   1 hr 35 mins

SERVES 4

INGREDIENTS

2 tbsp vegetable oil

4 chicken portions (about 225 g/8 oz each)

2 leeks, sliced

1 garlic clove, crushed

4 tbsp plain flour

850 ml/1½ pints chicken stock

300 ml/10 fl oz dry white wine

125 g/4¼ oz baby carrots, halved lengthways

125 g/4¼ oz baby sweetcorn cobs, halved lengthways

450 g/1 lb small new potatoes

1 bouquet garni sachet

150 ml/5 fl oz double cream

salt and pepper

1 Heat the oil in a large frying pan. Cook the chicken for 10 minutes, turning until browned. Transfer to a casserole dish using a perforated spoon.

2 Add the leek and garlic and cook for 2–3 minutes, stirring. Stir in the flour, cook for another minute and remove from the heat. Stir in stock and wine, and season.

3 Return the pan to the heat and bring to the boil. Stir in the carrots, sweetcorn, potatoes and bouquet garni. Transfer the mixture to the casserole dish.

4 Cover and cook in a preheated oven, 180°C/350°F/Gas Mark 4, for 1 hour.

5 Remove the casserole to stir in the cream, return to the oven uncovered, and cook for 15 minutes. Remove the bouquet garni, season, and serve with rice.

COOK'S TIP

Use turkey fillets instead of the chicken, if preferred, and vary the vegetables according to those you have to hand.

Potato, Leek & Chicken Pie

This pie has an attractive filo pastry case with a ruffled top made from strips of the pastry brushed with melted butter.

NUTRITIONAL INFORMATION

Calories 543	Sugars 7g	
Protein 21g	Fat 27g	
Carbohydrate . . .56g	Saturates 16g	

 15 mins   1 hr 5 mins

SERVES 4

I N G R E D I E N T S

225 g/8 oz waxy potatoes, cubed

5 tbsp butter

1 skinned chicken breast fillet (about 175 g/6 oz), cubed

1 leek, sliced

150 g/5½ oz chestnut mushrooms, sliced

2½ tbsp plain flour

300 ml/10 fl oz milk

1 tbsp Dijon mustard

2 tbsp chopped fresh sage

225 g/8 oz filo pastry, thawed if frozen

3 tbsp butter, melted

salt and pepper

1 Cook the cubed potato in a saucepan of boiling water for 5 minutes; drain.

2 Melt the butter in a frying pan and cook the chicken cubes for 5 minutes.

3 Add the leek and mushrooms and cook for 3 minutes, stirring. Stir in the flour and cook for 1 minute. Gradually add the milk and bring to the boil. Add the mustard, sage and potatoes, season, then leave the mixture to simmer for 10 minutes.

4 Meanwhile, line a deep pie dish with half of the sheets of filo pastry. Spoon

the sauce into the dish and cover with one sheet of pastry. Brush the pastry with butter and lay another sheet on top. Brush this sheet with more butter.

5 Cut the remaining filo pastry into strips and fold them onto the top of the pie creating a ruffled effect. Brush the strips with the melted butter and cook in a preheated oven, 180˚C/350˚F/Gas Mark 4, for 45 minutes, or until crisp. Serve hot.

COOK'S TIP

If the top of the pie starts to brown too quickly, cover it with foil halfway through the cooking time to allow the pastry base to cook through without the top burning.

Chicken Suprêmes Nellwyn

The refreshing combination of chicken and orange sauce with wholemeal spaghetti makes this a perfect dish for a warm summer evening.

NUTRITIONAL INFORMATION

Calories 933   Sugars 34g
Protein . . . . .74g   Fat 24g
Carbohydrate . .100g   Saturates 5g

10 mins   35 mins

SERVES 4

INGREDIENTS

2 tbsp rapeseed oil

3 tbsp olive oil

4 x 225 g/8 oz chicken suprêmes

150 ml/5 fl oz orange brandy

2 tbsp plain flour

150 ml/5 fl oz freshly-squeezed
   orange juice

25 g/1 oz courgette, cut into matchstick
   strips

25 g/1 oz red pepper, cut into matchstick
   strips

25 g/1 oz leek, finely shredded

salt and pepper

400 g/14 oz dried wholemeal spaghetti

3 large oranges, peeled and cut
   into segments

1 orange, rind cut into very fine strips

2 tbsp chopped fresh tarragon

150 ml/5 fl oz fromage frais or
   ricotta cheese

fresh tarragon leaves, to garnish

1 Heat the rapeseed oil and 1 tbsp of the olive oil in a frying pan. Add the chicken and cook quickly until golden brown. Add the orange brandy and cook for 3 minutes. Sprinkle over the flour and cook for 2 minutes.

2 Lower the heat and add the orange juice, courgette, pepper and leek and season to taste. Simmer for 5 minutes, or until the sauce has thickened.

3 Meanwhile, bring a pan of salted water to the boil. Add the spaghetti and 1 tbsp of the olive oil and cook for 10 minutes. Drain, transfer to a serving dish and drizzle over the remaining oil.

4 Add half the orange segments, half the orange rind, the tarragon and fromage frais or ricotta cheese to the sauce in the pan and cook for 3 minutes.

5 Place the chicken on top of the spaghetti, pour a little sauce over it, garnish with the remaining orange segments, rind and tarragon, and serve immediately.

Chicken & Lobster on Penne

This dish provides a touch of luxury for the tastebuds, yet it is not extravagant because it uses just a small amount of lobster.

NUTRITIONAL INFORMATION

Calories	696	Sugars	.........4g
Protein	........59g	Fat	..........32g
Carbohydrate	...45g	Saturates	.......9g

 10 mins   45 mins

SERVES 6

I N G R E D I E N T S

butter, for greasing

6 chicken breasts

450 g/1 lb dried penne rigati

6 tbsp extra virgin olive oil

90 g/3¼ oz freshly grated
  Parmesan cheese

FILLING

115 g/4 oz lobster meat, chopped

2 shallots, very finely chopped

2 figs, chopped

1 tbsp garam marsala

2 tbsp breadcrumbs

1 large egg, beaten

salt and pepper

1 Grease 6 pieces of kitchen foil, which are large enough to enclose the chicken breasts, and lightly grease a baking sheet.

2 Place all of the filling ingredients into a mixing bowl and blend together thoroughly with a spoon.

3 Cut a pocket in each chicken breast with a sharp knife and fill with the lobster mixture. Wrap the chicken in the foil, place the parcels on the greased baking sheet and bake in a preheated oven at 200°C/400°F/Gas 6 for 30 minutes.

4 Meanwhile, bring a large pan of lightly salted water to the boil. Add the pasta and 1 tbsp of the olive oil and cook for about 10 minutes, or until tender but still firm to the bite. Drain the pasta thoroughly and transfer to a large serving plate. Sprinkle the remaining olive oil and the grated Parmesan cheese, over it, set aside and keep warm.

5 Carefully remove the foil from around the chicken breasts. Slice the breasts very thinly, arrange them over the pasta and serve immediately.

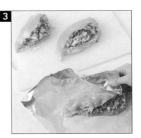

COOK'S TIP

The cut of chicken known as suprême consists of the breast and wing. It is always skinned.

Pan-cooked Chicken

Artichokes are a familiar ingredient in traditional Italian cookery. In this dish, they are used to delicately flavour chicken breasts.

NUTRITIONAL INFORMATION

Calories 296   Sugars 2g
Protein . . . . .27g   Fat 15g
Carbohydrate . . . .7g   Saturates 6g

 15 mins   55 mins

SERVES 4

INGREDIENTS

4 chicken breasts, part-boned

salt and pepper

2 tbsp olive oil

2 tbsp butter

2 red onions, cut into wedges

2 tbsp lemon juice

150 ml/5 fl oz dry white wine

150 ml/5 fl oz chicken stock

2 tsp plain flour

400 g/14 oz can artichoke halves,
    drained and halved

chopped fresh parsley, to garnish

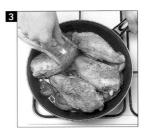

1 Season the chicken with salt and pepper to taste. Heat the oil and 1 tablespoon of the butter in a large frying pan. Add the chicken and fry for 4–5 minutes on each side, or until lightly golden. Remove from the pan using a slotted spoon.

2 Toss the onion in lemon juice and add to the frying pan. Fry gently, stirring, for 3–4 minutes, or until it just softens.

3 Return the partly cooked chicken to the pan. Pour in the wine and stock, bring to the boil, cover and simmer gently for 30 minutes.

4 Remove the chicken from the pan. Carefully reserve the cooking juices, and keep them warm to one side. Bring the juices to the boil, and boil rapidly for 5 minutes.

5 Blend the remaining butter with the flour to form a paste. Reduce the reserved warm juices to a simmer and spoon the paste into the frying pan, stirring until thickened.

6 Adjust the seasoning according to taste, stir in the artichoke hearts and cook for a further 2 minutes. Pour the mixture over the chicken and garnish with chopped parsley.

Italian Chicken Parcels

This cooking method makes the chicken aromatic and succulent, and because the ingredients cook in their own juices it uses a minimum of oil.

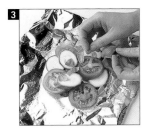

NUTRITIONAL INFORMATION

Calories	234	Sugars	.........5g
Protein	........28g	Fat	..........12g
Carbohydrate	....5g	Saturates	.......5g

 20 mins   30 mins

SERVES 6

I N G R E D I E N T S

1 tbsp olive oil

6 skinless chicken breast fillets

250 g/9 oz Mozzarella cheese

500 g/1 lb 2 oz courgettes, sliced

6 large tomatoes, sliced

1 small bunch fresh basil or oregano

pepper

rice or pasta, to serve

1 Cut 6 pieces of kitchen foil, each piece measuring approximately 25 cm/10 inches square. Brush the foil squares lightly with olive oil and set aside until required.

2 With a sharp knife, slash each chicken breast at regular intervals. Slice the Mozzarella cheese and place between the cuts in the chicken.

3 Divide the courgettes and tomatoes between the pieces of foil and sprinkle with pepper to taste. Tear or roughly chop the basil or oregano and scatter over the vegetables in each parcel.

4 Place the chicken on top of each pile of vegetables, season with pepper, then wrap in the foil to enclose the chicken and vegetables, tucking in the ends.

5 Place on a baking tray and bake in a preheated oven, 200°C/400°C/Gas Mark 6, for about 30 minutes.

6 To serve, unwrap each foil parcel and serve with rice or pasta.

COOK'S TIP
To aid cooking, place the vegetables and chicken on the shiny side of the foil. This ensures that the heat is absorbed into the parcel and not reflected away from it.

Parma-wrapped Chicken

Stuffed with ricotta, nutmeg and spinach, and wrapped in wafer-thin slices of Parma ham, this chicken is then cooked gently in white wine.

NUTRITIONAL INFORMATION

Calories 426   Sugars 4g
Protein ....44g   Fat 21g
Carbohydrate ....9g   Saturates 8g

20 mins   40 mins

SERVES 4

INGREDIENTS

125 g/4¼ oz frozen spinach, defrosted

125 g/4¼ oz ricotta cheese

pinch of grated nutmeg

salt and pepper

4 skinless, boneless chicken breasts (each weighing about 175 g/6 oz)

4 Parma ham slices

2 tbsp butter

1 tbsp olive oil

12 small onions or shallots

125 g/4½ oz button mushrooms, sliced

1 tbsp plain flour

150 ml/5 fl oz dry white or red wine

300 ml/10 fl oz chicken stock

1 Put the spinach into a sieve and press out the water with a spoon. Mix with the ricotta and nutmeg and season with salt and pepper to taste.

2 Using a sharp knife, slit each chicken breast through the side and enlarge each cut to form a pocket. Fill each cut with the spinach mixture, reshape the chicken breasts to enclose the mixture, wrap each breast tightly in a slice of ham and secure with cocktail sticks. Cover and chill in the refrigerator.

3 Heat the butter and oil in a frying pan and brown the chicken breasts for at least 2 minutes on each side. Transfer the chicken to a large, shallow ovenproof dish and keep warm until required.

4 Fry the onions and mushrooms for 2–3 minutes, or until lightly browned. Stir in the plain flour, then gradually add the wine and stock. Bring

to the boil, stirring constantly. Season with salt and pepper to taste and spoon the mixture around the chicken.

5 Cook the chicken uncovered in a preheated oven, 200°C/400°F/ Gas Mark 6, for 20 minutes. Turn the breasts over and cook for a further 10 minutes. Remove the cocktail sticks and serve with the sauce, together with carrot purée and green beans, if desired.

Chicken Risotto Milanese

This simple chicken risotto is one of Italy's best-known dishes, served in restaurants all over the world. But every cook varies the recipe slightly.

NUTRITIONAL INFORMATION

Calories 857	Sugars 1g	
Protein 57g	Fat 38g	
Carbohydrate . . .72g	Saturates 21g	

 5 mins   1 hr 5 mins

SERVES 4

I N G R E D I E N T S

125 g/4¼ oz butter

900 g/2 lb chicken, sliced thinly

1 large onion, chopped

500 g/1 lb 2 oz risotto rice

600 ml/1 pint chicken stock

150 ml/5 fl oz white wine

1 tsp crumbled saffron

salt and pepper

60 g/2¼ oz grated Parmesan cheese, to serve

1 Heat 4 tbsp of butter in a deep frying pan, and fry the chicken and onion until golden brown.

2 Add the rice to the frying pan, stir well, and cook for 15 minutes.

3 Heat the stock until boiling and gradually add to the rice. Add the white wine, saffron, salt and pepper and mix well. Simmer gently for 20 minutes, stirring occasionally, and adding more stock if the risotto becomes too dry.

4 Leave the risotto to stand for 2–3 minutes and just before serving, add a little more stock and simmer for 10 minutes. Serve the risotto, sprinkled with the grated Parmesan cheese and the remaining butter.

Kung Po Chicken

Cashew nuts are a principal ingredient in this traditional Szechuan recipe, but peanuts, walnuts or almonds may be used instead.

NUTRITIONAL INFORMATION

Calories . . . . . . .294 Sugars 3g
Protein . . . . .21g Fat 18g
Carbohydrate . . .10g Saturates 4g

 10 mins   10 mins

SERVES 4

I N G R E D I E N T S

250–300 g/9–10½ oz chicken meat, boned and skinned

¼ tsp salt

⅓ egg white

1 tsp cornflour paste
  (see page 39)

1 green pepper, cored and seeded

4 tbsp vegetable oil

1 spring onion, cut into short sections

1 cm/½ inch fresh ginger root, sliced

4–5 small dried red chillies, soaked, deseeded and shredded

2 tbsp crushed yellow bean sauce

1 tsp rice wine or dry sherry

125 g/4¼ oz roasted cashew nuts

drops of sesame oil

boiled rice, to serve

1 Cut the chicken into small cubes about the size of sugar cubes. Place the chicken in a small bowl and mix with a pinch of salt, the egg white and the cornflour paste, in that order.

2 Cut the green pepper into cubes or triangles about the same size as the chicken pieces.

3 Heat the oil in a wok, add the chicken and stir-fry for 1 minute. Remove the chicken with a slotted spoon and keep warm.

4 Add the spring onion, ginger, chillies and green pepper. Stir-fry for 1 minute, then add the chicken with the yellow bean sauce and wine. Blend well and stir-fry for another minute. Finally stir in the cashew nuts and sesame oil. Serve hot with boiled rice.

VARIATION

Any nuts can be used in place of the cashew nuts. The important point is the crunchy texture, which is very much a feature of Szechuan cooking.

Lemon Chicken

This is on everyone's list of favourite Chinese dishes, perhaps because it is so simple to make. Serve it with stir-fried vegetables for a delicious meal.

NUTRITIONAL INFORMATION

Calories 272	Sugars 1g
Protein 36g	Fat 11g
Carbohydrate 5g	Saturates 2g

 5 mins   15 mins

SERVES 4

INGREDIENTS

vegetable oil, for deep-frying

650 g/1 lb 7 oz skinless, boneless chicken, cut into strips

SAUCE

1 tbsp cornflour

6 tbsp cold water

3 tbsp fresh lemon juice

2 tbsp sweet sherry

½ tsp caster sugar

GARNISH

lemon slices

shredded spring onion

1 Heat the oil for deep-frying in a wok or frying pan to 180°C/350°F or until a bread cube browns in 30 seconds.

2 Reduce the heat and stir-fry the chicken strips for 3–4 minutes, or until cooked through.

3 Remove the chicken with a slotted spoon, set aside and keep warm. Drain the oil from the wok.

4 To make the sauce, mix the cornflour with 2 tablespoons of the water to form a paste.

5 Pour the lemon juice and remaining water into the mixture in the wok.

6 Add the sweet sherry and caster sugar and bring to the boil, stirring until the sugar has completely dissolved.

7 Stir in the cornflour sauce and return to the boil. Reduce the heat and simmer, stirring constantly, for 2–3 minutes, or until the sauce is thickened and clear.

8 Transfer the chicken to a warm serving plate and pour the sauce over the top. Garnish with the lemon slices and shredded spring onion and serve immediately.

COOK'S TIP

If you would prefer to use chicken portions rather than strips, cook them in the oil, covered, over a low heat for about 30 minutes, or until cooked through.

Peanut Sesame Chicken

Sesame seeds and peanuts give extra crunch and flavour to this stir-fry, and the fruit juice glaze gives the sauce a glossy coating.

NUTRITIONAL INFORMATION

Calories	435	Sugars 10g
Protein	........38g	Fat 26g
Carbohydrate	...14g	Saturates 4g

🥔 10 mins   🕐 15 mins

SERVES 4

INGREDIENTS

2 tbsp vegetable oil

2 tbsp sesame oil

500 g/1 lb 2 oz boneless, skinned chicken breasts, sliced into strips

250 g/9 oz broccoli, divided into small florets

250 g/9 oz baby or dwarf corn, halved if large

1 small red pepper, cored, deseeded and sliced

2 tbsp soy sauce

250 ml/9 fl oz orange juice

2 tsp cornflour

2 tbsp sesame seeds, toasted

60 g/2¼ oz roasted, shelled, unsalted peanuts

rice or noodles, to serve

COOK'S TIP

Make sure you use the unsalted variety of peanuts or the dish will be too salty, as the soy sauce adds extra saltiness.

1 Heat the oils in a large, heavy-based frying pan or wok until smoking. Add the chicken strips and stir-fry for about 4–5 minutes, or until browned.

2 Add the broccoli, corn and red pepper and stir-fry over a high heat for another 1–2 minutes until they just soften.

3 Meanwhile, mix the soy sauce together with the orange juice and the cornflour. Stir into the chicken and vegetable mixture, stirring constantly until the sauce has slightly thickened and a glaze develops.

4 Stir in the sesame seeds and peanuts, mixing well. Heat the stir-fry for a further 3–4 minutes.

5 Transfer the stir-fry to a warm serving dish and serve with rice or noodles.

Braised Chicken

A glaze served with the chicken as a sauce gives this straightforward whole chicken dish a professional touch.

NUTRITIONAL INFORMATION

Calories 294   Sugars 9g
Protein . . . . .31g   Fat 15g
Carbohydrate . . .10g   Saturates 3g

 10 mins   1 hr 15 mins

SERVES 4

I N G R E D I E N T S

1.5 kg/3 lb 5 oz chicken

3 tbsp vegetable oil

1 tbsp peanut oil

2 tbsp dark brown sugar

5 tbsp dark soy sauce

150 ml/5 fl oz water

2 garlic cloves, crushed

1 small onion, chopped

1 fresh red chilli, chopped

celery leaves and chives, to garnish

1 Preheat a large wok or large frying pan in preparation.

2 Clean the chicken inside and out with damp kitchen paper.

3 Place the vegetable oil and peanut oil in the wok, add the dark brown sugar and heat together gently until the sugar caramelizes.

4 Stir the soy sauce into the wok. Add the chicken and turn it in the mixture to coat thoroughly on all sides.

5 Add the water, crushed garlic, chopped onion and chopped chilli. Cover and simmer, turning the chicken

occasionally, for about 1 hour, or until cooked through. Test by piercing a thigh with the point of a knife or a skewer – if the juices run clear, the chicken is cooked.

6 Remove the chicken from the wok and set it to aside. Increase the heat and reduce the sauce in the wok until it has thickened. Transfer the chicken to a serving plate, garnish with celery leaves and chives and serve with the sauce.

COOK'S TIP

For a spicier sauce, add 1 tbsp of finely chopped fresh root ginger and 1 tbsp ground Szechuan peppercorns with the chilli in Step 5.

Chicken & Rice Casserole

This is a quick-cooking, spicy casserole of rice, chicken and vegetables in an aromatic liquor flavoured with soy and ginger.

NUTRITIONAL INFORMATION

Calories	502	Sugars	........2g
Protein	........55g	Fat	..........9g
Carbohydrate	...52g	Saturates	.......3g

 15 mins, plus 30 mins to marinate   45 mins

SERVES 4

INGREDIENTS

150 g/5½ oz long-grain rice

1 tbsp dry sherry

2 tbsp light soy sauce

2 tbsp dark soy sauce

2 tsp dark brown sugar

1 tsp salt

1 tsp sesame oil

900 g/2 lb skinless, boneless chicken, diced

850 ml/1½ pints chicken stock

2 open-cap mushrooms, sliced

60 g/2¼ oz water chestnuts, halved

75 g/2¾ oz broccoli florets

1 yellow pepper, sliced

4 tsp grated fresh root ginger

whole chives, to garnish

1 Cook the rice in boiling water for 15 minutes. Drain well, rinse under cold water and drain again thoroughly.

2 Mix together the sherry, soy sauces, sugar, salt and sesame oil.

3 Stir the chicken into the soy mixture, turning to coat the chicken well. Leave to marinate for about 30 minutes.

4 Bring the stock to the boil in a saucepan or wok. Add the chicken with the marinade, mushrooms, water chestnuts, broccoli, pepper and ginger.

5 Stir in the rice, reduce the heat, cover and cook for 25-30 minutes, or until the chicken and vegetables are cooked through. Transfer to serving plates, garnish with chives and serve.

VARIATION

This dish would work equally well with beef or pork. Chinese dried mushrooms may be used instead of the open-cap mushrooms, if rehydrated before adding to the dish.

Sage Chicken & Rice

Cooking in a single pot means all of the flavours are retained. This is a substantial meal, needing only a salad and some crusty bread.

NUTRITIONAL INFORMATION

Calories 247	Sugars 5g	
Protein 26g	Fat 5g	
Carbohydrate ...25g	Saturates 2g	

 15 mins   45 mins

SERVES 4

INGREDIENTS

1 large onion, chopped

1 garlic clove, crushed

2 celery sticks, sliced

2 carrots, diced

2 sprigs fresh sage

300 ml/10 fl oz chicken stock

350 g/12 oz boneless, skinless chicken breasts

225 g/8 oz mixed brown and wild rice

400 g/14 oz can chopped tomatoes

dash of Tabasco sauce

2 courgettes, trimmed and thinly sliced

100 g/3½ oz lean ham, diced

salt and pepper

fresh sage, to garnish

TO SERVE

salad leaves

crusty bread

1 Place the pieces of onion, garlic, celery, carrots and sprigs of fresh sage in a large saucepan and pour in the chicken stock.

2 Bring the vegetable and herb mixture to the boil, cover the pan and allow to simmer for 5 minutes.

3 Cut the chicken into 2.5 cm/1 inch cubes and stir into the pan with the vegetables. Cover the pan and continue to cook for a further 5 minutes.

4 Stir in the mixed brown and wild rice and chopped tomatoes.

5 Add a dash of Tabasco sauce to taste and season well. Bring to the boil, cover and simmer for 25 minutes.

6 Carefully stir in the sliced courgettes and diced ham and continue to cook, uncovered, for a further 10 minutes, stirring occasionally, until the rice is just tender.

7 Remove the sprigs of sage and then discard them.

8 Garnish with sage leaves and serve with a salad and fresh crusty bread.

Chilli Chicken Meatballs

These tender chicken and sweetcorn nuggets are served with a sweet and sour sauce. They make great nibbles for cocktails or for a party.

NUTRITIONAL INFORMATION

Calories 196	Sugars 12g
Protein 26g	Fat 4g
Carbohydrate ...15g	Saturates 1g

30 mins   25 mins

SERVES 4

INGREDIENTS

450 g/1 lb lean chicken, minced

4 spring onions, trimmed and finely chopped, plus extra to garnish

1 small red chilli, deseeded and finely chopped

2.5 cm/1 inch piece root ginger, finely chopped

100 g/3½ oz can sweetcorn (no added sugar or salt), drained

salt and white pepper

boiled jasmine rice, to serve

SAUCE

150 ml/5 fl oz fresh chicken stock (see page 5)

100 g/3½ oz cubed pineapple in natural juice, drained, with 4 tbsp reserved juice

1 carrot, cut into thin strips

1 small red pepper, deseeded and diced, plus extra to garnish

1 small green pepper, deseeded and diced

1 tbsp light soy sauce

2 tbsp rice vinegar

1 tbsp caster sugar

1 tbsp tomato purée

2 tsp cornflour mixed to a paste with 4 tsp cold water

1 To make the meatballs, place the chicken in a bowl and mix with the spring onions, chilli, ginger, sweetcorn and salt and pepper.

2 Divide into 16 portions and form each into a ball. Bring a saucepan of water to the boil. Arrange the meatballs on baking paper in a steamer or large sieve, place over the water, cover and steam for 10–12 minutes.

3 To make the sauce, pour the stock and pineapple juice into a pan and bring to the boil. Add the carrot and peppers, cover and simmer for 5 minutes. Add the remaining ingredients, stirring until thickened. Season and set aside.

4 Drain the meatballs and transfer to a serving plate. Garnish with snipped chives and serve with boiled rice and the sauce (reheated if necessary).

Crispy Stuffed Chicken

An attractive main course of chicken breasts filled with mixed peppers and set on a sea of red peppers and rich tomato sauce.

NUTRITIONAL INFORMATION

Calories 196   Sugars 4g
Protein . . . . .29g   Fat 6g
Carbohydrate . . . .6g   Saturates 2g

20 mins   50 mins

SERVES 4

I N G R E D I E N T S

4 boneless chicken breasts (about 150 g/5½ oz each), skinned

salt and pepper

4 sprigs fresh tarragon

½ small orange pepper, deseeded and sliced

½ small green pepper, deseeded and sliced

15 g/½ oz wholemeal breadcrumbs

1 tbsp sesame seeds

4 tbsp lemon juice

1 small red pepper, halved and deseeded

200 g/7 oz can chopped tomatoes

1 small red chilli, deseeded and chopped

¼ tsp celery salt

fresh tarragon, to garnish

1 Preheat the oven to 200°C/400°F/Gas Mark 6. Make a slit in the chicken breasts with a small, sharp knife to create a pocket in each.

2 Season each pocket and place a tarragon sprig and the slices of orange and green peppers inside. Place the chicken breasts on a non-stick baking tray and sprinkle breadcrumbs and sesame seeds over them.

3 Spoon 1 tablespoon lemon juice over each chicken breast and bake in the oven for 35–40 minutes, or until the chicken is tender and cooked through.

4 Meanwhile, preheat the grill to a hot setting. Arrange the red pepper halves, skin side up, on the rack and cook under the hot grill for 5–6 minutes, or until the skin blisters. Leave to cool for 10 minutes, then peel off the skins.

5 Put the red pepper in a blender, add the tomatoes, chilli and celery salt and process for a few seconds. Season to taste. Alternatively, finely chop the red pepper and press through a sieve with the tomatoes and chilli.

6 When the chicken is cooked, heat the sauce, spoon a little onto a warm plate and arrange a chicken breast in the centre. Garnish with tarragon and serve.

Chicken with a Yogurt Crust

A spicy, Indian-style coating is baked around lean chicken to give a full flavour. Serve with a tomato, cucumber and coriander relish.

NUTRITIONAL INFORMATION

Calories	176	Sugars	.........5g
Protein	........30g	Fat	..........4g
Carbohydrate	....5g	Saturates	......1g

 10 mins   35 mins

SERVES 4

I N G R E D I E N T S

1 garlic clove, crushed

2.5 cm/1 inch piece root ginger, finely chopped

1 fresh green chilli, deseeded and finely chopped

6 tbsp low-fat natural yogurt

1 tbsp tomato purée

1 tsp ground turmeric

1 tsp garam masala

1 tbsp lime juice

4 boneless, skinless chicken breasts (each 125 g/4¼ oz)

salt and pepper

wedges of lime or lemon, to serve

R E L I S H

4 tomatoes

¼ cucumber

1 small red onion

2 tbsp fresh, chopped coriander

1 Preheat the oven to 190°C/375°F/Gas Mark 5 and have ready a mixing bowl and a baking sheet.

2 Place the garlic, ginger, chilli, yogurt, tomato purée, spices, lime juice and seasoning in a bowl and mix to combine all the ingredients.

3 Wash and pat dry the chicken breasts thoroughly with absorbent kitchen paper and place them on a baking sheet.

4 Brush or spread the spicy yogurt mix over the chicken and bake in the oven for 30–35 minutes, or until the meat is tender and cooked through.

5 Meanwhile, make the relish. Finely chop the tomatoes, cucumber and onion and mix together with the coriander. Season with salt and pepper to taste, cover and chill in the refrigerator until required.

6 Drain the cooked chicken on absorbent kitchen paper and serve hot with the relish and lemon or lime wedges. Alternatively, allow to cool, chill for at least 1 hour and serve sliced as part of a salad.

Lemon & Honey Chicken

A good dish for the barbecue, this sweet, citrus-scented chicken can be served hot or cold. Sesame-flavoured noodles are the ideal accompaniment.

NUTRITIONAL INFORMATION

Calories 398   Sugars 8g
Protein . . . . .34g   Fat 5g
Carbohydrate . . .54g   Saturates 1g

15 mins   30 mins

SERVES 4

I N G R E D I E N T S

4 boneless chicken breasts (about 125 g/4¼ oz each)

2 tbsp clear honey

1 tbsp dark soy sauce

1 tsp lemon rind, finely grated

1 tbsp lemon juice

salt and pepper

N O O D L E S

225 g/8 oz rice noodles

2 tsp sesame oil

1 tbsp sesame seeds

1 tsp lemon rind, finely grated

T O G A R N I S H

1 tbsp fresh chives, chopped

lemon rind, finely grated

1 Preheat the grill to medium. Skin and trim the chicken breasts to remove any excess fat, then wash and pat them dry with absorbent kitchen paper. Using a sharp knife, score the chicken breasts with a criss-cross pattern on both sides (making sure that you do not cut all the way through the meat).

2 Mix together the honey, soy sauce, lemon rind and juice in a small bowl, and then season well with black pepper.

3 Arrange the chicken breasts on the grill rack so that they do not overlap and brush with half the honey mixture. Cook for 10 minutes, turn over and brush with the remaining mixture. Cook for a further 8–10 minutes or until cooked through.

4 Meanwhile, prepare the noodles according to the instructions on the packet. Drain well and pile into a warm serving bowl. Mix the noodles with the sesame oil, sesame seeds and the lemon rind. Season and keep warm.

5 Drain the chicken and serve with a small mound of noodles. Garnish the final arrangement with chopped chives and lemon zest.

VARIATION

For a different flavour, replace the lemon with orange or lime. If you prefer, serve the chicken with boiled rice or pasta, which you can flavour with sesame seeds and citrus rind in the same way.

Harlequin Chicken

This colourful dish will tempt the appetites of all the family. Toddlers enjoy the fun shapes of the multicoloured peppers

NUTRITIONAL INFORMATION

Calories	183	Sugar 8g
Protein	........24g	Fats 6g
Carbohydrates	....8g	Saturates 1g

5 mins   25 mins

SERVES 4

INGREDIENTS

10 skinless, boneless chicken thighs

1 onion

1 each red, green and yellow peppers

1 tbsp sunflower oil

400 g/14 oz can chopped tomatoes

2 tbsp chopped fresh parsley

pepper

wholemeal bread and salad, to serve

1 Using a sharp knife, cut the chicken thighs into bite-sized pieces.

2 Peel and thinly slice the onion. Halve and deseed the peppers and cut into small diamond shapes.

COOK'S TIP

If you are making this dish for small children, the chicken can be finely chopped or minced first.

3 Heat the sunflower oil in a shallow pan, and when it is hot enough to begin smoking, quickly fry the chicken and onion until they are golden.

4 Add the peppers, cook the mixture for 2–3 minutes, then stir in the tomatoes and chopped fresh parsley and season the chicken and vegetables with pepper to taste.

5 Cover the pan tightly and simmer for approximately 15 minutes, until the chicken and vegetables are tender. Remove from the pan and serve the Harlequin Chicken hot with wholemeal bread and a green salad.

Chicken with Vermouth

The sauce for this dish is based on the aromatic flavours of vermouth, and the chicken is partnered with refreshing grapes.

NUTRITIONAL INFORMATION

Calories 271	Sugars 5g
Protein 31g	Fat 4g
Carbohydrate . . .22g	Saturates 1g

🥔 10 mins   🕐 45 mins

SERVES 4

I N G R E D I E N T S

4 x 175 g/6 oz part-boned chicken breasts, skinned

150 ml/5 fl oz white vermouth

150 ml/5 fl oz fresh chicken stock (see page 5)

2 shallots, sliced thinly

400 g/14 oz can artichoke hearts, drained and halved

125 g/4¼ oz seedless green grapes

1 tbsp cornflour mixed with 1 tbsp cold water

salt and pepper

watercress sprigs, to garnish

freshly cooked vegetables, to serve

1 Cook the chicken in a heavy-based non-stick frying pan for 2–3 minutes on each side until sealed. Drain on kitchen paper.

2 Rinse out the pan, then add the dry vermouth and stock. Bring to the boil and add the shallots and chicken.

3 Cover and simmer for 35 minutes. Season with salt and pepper according to taste.

4 Carefully stir in the artichokes and the grapes and then heat through for 2–3 minutes.

5 Stir in the cornflour mixture until thickened. Garnish the chicken with watercress sprigs and serve with freshly cooked vegetables.

COOK'S TIP

Vermouth is a mixture of wines. It is fortified, and enriched with a secret blend of herbs and spices. It is available in sweet and dry forms. Dry white wine would make a suitable substitute in this recipe.

Cheesy Baked Chicken

Cheese and mustard, and a simple, crispy coating, make a delicious combination in this healthy dish of low-fat ingredients.

NUTRITIONAL INFORMATION

Calories 225	Sugars 1g
Protein 32g	Fat 7g
Carbohydrate 9g	Saturates 3g

5 mins   35 mins

SERVES 4

INGREDIENTS

1 tbsp skimmed milk

2 tbsp English mustard

60 g/2¼ oz grated low-fat mature Cheddar cheese

3 tbsp plain flour

2 tbsp chopped fresh chives

4 skinless, boneless chicken breasts

TO SERVE

jacket potatoes and fresh vegetables

crisp salad

1 Mix together the milk and mustard in a bowl. Mix the cheese with the flour and chives on a plate.

2 Dip the chicken into the milk and mustard mixture, brushing with a pastry brush to coat evenly.

3 Dip the chicken breasts into the cheese mixture, pressing to coat them evenly all over.

4 Place on a baking tray and spoon any spare cheese coating on top.

5 Bake the chicken in a preheated oven, at 200°C/400°F/Gas Mark 6, for 30–35 minutes, or until golden brown and the juices run clear, not pink, when the chicken is pierced to the centre with a skewer.

6 Serve the chicken hot, with jacket potatoes and fresh vegetables, or serve cold, with a crisp salad.

COOK'S TIP

Part-boned chicken breasts are very suitable for pan-cooking and casseroling, as they stay moist and tender. Try using chicken quarters if part-boned breasts are unavailable.

Fragrant Spiced Chicken

The mixture of chicken and chickpeas in this dish is particularly tasty and nutritious. Use canned chickpeas for a quick meal.

NUTRITIONAL INFORMATION

Calories ...... .343 Sugars 5g
Protein ....28g Fat .... .16g
Carbohydrate ...24g Saturates 3g

 10 mins   30 mins

SERVES 4

I N G R E D I E N T S

3 tbsp ghee or vegetable oil

8 small chicken portions, such as thighs or drumsticks

1 large onion, peeled and chopped

2 garlic cloves, peeled and crushed

1–2 fresh green chillies, deseeded and chopped, or 1–2 tsp minced chilli (from a jar)

2 tsp ground cumin

2 tsp ground coriander

1 tsp garam masala

1 tsp ground turmeric

400 g/14 oz can chopped tomatoes

150 ml/5 fl oz water

1 tbsp chopped fresh mint

400 g/14 oz can chickpeas, drained

salt

1 tbsp chopped fresh coriander

low-fat natural yogurt, to serve (optional)

1 Heat the ghee or oil in a large saucepan and fry the chicken until sealed all over and lightly golden.

2 Remove from the pan. Add the onion, garlic, chilli and spices and cook very gently for 2 minutes, stirring frequently.

3 Stir in the tomatoes, water, mint and chickpeas. Mix thoroughly, return the chicken portions to the pan, season with salt, then cover and simmer gently for about 20 minutes, or until the chicken is tender.

4 Taste and adjust the seasoning, then sprinkle with the coriander and serve hot with yogurt, if using.

VARIATION

Canned black-eyed beans and red kidney beans also make delicious additions to this spicy chicken dish. Be sure to drain and rinse canned beans before adding to the pan.

Chicken & Chilli Bean Pot

This aromatic chicken dish has a spicy Mexican kick. Chicken thighs have a wonderful flavour when cooked in this Latin American way.

NUTRITIONAL INFORMATION

Calories 333   Sugars 10g
Protein ....25g   Fat 13g
Carbohydrate ...32g   Saturates 2g

10 mins   40 mins

SERVES 4

INGREDIENTS

2 tbsp plain flour

1 tsp chili powder

8 chicken thighs or 4 chicken legs

3 tbsp vegetable oil

2 garlic cloves, crushed

1 large onion, chopped

1 green or red pepper, deseeded
    and chopped

300 ml/10 fl oz chicken stock

350 g/12 oz tomatoes, chopped

400 g/14 oz can red kidney beans, rinsed
    and drained

2 tbsp tomato purée

salt and pepper

1 Mix the flour, chilli powder and seasoning in a shallow dish. Rinse the chicken, then dip it into the seasoned flour, turning to coat it on all sides.

2 Heat the oil in a pan, add the chicken, and brown for 3–4 minutes, turning.

3 Lift the chicken out of the pan kitchen paper.

4 Add the garlic, onion and pepper to the pan and cook for 2–3 minutes, or until softened.

5 Add the stock, tomatoes, kidney beans and tomato purée, stirring well. Bring to the boil, then return the chicken to the pan. Reduce the heat and simmer, covered, for about 30 minutes, or until the chicken is tender. Season and serve at once.

COOK'S TIP

For extra intensity of flavour, use sun-dried tomato paste instead of ordinary tomato purée.

Lemon & Tarragon Poussins

Grilled spatchcocked poussins, or baby chickens, are complemented by the delicate fragrance of lemon and tarragon.

NUTRITIONAL INFORMATION

Calories 449	Sugars 2g	
Protein 38g	Fat 30g	
Carbohydrate 5g	Saturates 10g	

 15 mins   35 mins

SERVES 2

INGREDIENTS

2 poussins

4 sprigs fresh tarragon

1 tsp oil

2 tbsp butter

½ lemon rind

1 tbsp lemon juice

1 garlic clove, crushed

salt and pepper

tarragon and orange slices, to garnish

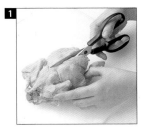

1 Prepare the poussins, turn them breast-side down on a chopping board and cut them through the backbone using kitchen scissors. Crush each bird gently to break the bones so that they lie flat while cooking. Season each with salt.

2 Turn them over and insert a sprig of tarragon under the skin over each side of the breast.

3 Brush the chickens with oil, using a pastry brush, and place under a preheated hot grill about 13 cm/ 5 inches from the heat. Grill the chickens for about 15 minutes, turning half way, until they are lightly browned.

4 To make the glaze for the chicken, melt the butter in a saucepan, add the lemon rind and juice and the garlic, and season to taste.

5 Brush the poussins with the glaze and cook for a further 15 minutes, turning them once and brushing regularly so that they stay moist. Garnish the chickens with tarragon and orange slices and serve with new potatoes.

COOK'S TIP

Once the poussins are flattened, insert 2 metal skewers through them to keep them flat.

Devilled Chicken

This succulent chicken is spiked with cayenne pepper and paprika, and finished off with a fruity, tangy sauce.

NUTRITIONAL INFORMATION

Calories 455   Sugars 19g
Protein . . . . .37g   Fat 23g
Carbohydrate . . .29g   Saturates 14g

 10 mins   35 mins

SERVES 2–3

INGREDIENTS

25 g/1 oz plain flour

1 tbsp cayenne pepper

1 tsp paprika

350 g/12 oz skinless, boneless chicken, diced

2 tbsp butter

1 onion, chopped finely

450 ml/16 fl oz milk, warmed

4 tbsp apple purée

125 g/4¼ oz green grapes

150 ml/5 fl oz soured cream

sprinkle of paprika

1 Mix the flour, cayenne pepper and paprika together and use the mixture to coat the chicken.

2 Shake off any excess flour. Melt the butter in a saucepan and gently fry the chicken with the onion for 4 minutes.

3 Stir in the flour and spice mixture. Add the milk slowly until thickened.

4 Simmer gently over a low heat until the sauce is smooth.

5 Add the apple purée and grapes and simmer gently for 20 minutes.

6 Transfer the chicken and devilled sauce to a serving dish and top with soured cream and a sprinkling of paprika before serving.

COOK'S TIP

Add more paprika if desired – as it is quite a mild spice, you can add plenty without it being too overpowering.

Golden Chicken Pilau

This is a simple version of a creamy and mildly spiced Indian pilau. There are many ingredients, but very little preparation is needed for this dish.

NUTRITIONAL INFORMATION

Calories	581	Sugars	.......22g
Protein	........31g	Fat	..........19g
Carbohydrate	...73g	Saturates	......12g

10 mins   20 mins

SERVES 4

I N G R E D I E N T S

4 tbsp butter

8 skinless, boneless chicken thighs,cut into large pieces

1 onion, sliced

1 tsp ground turmeric

1 tsp ground cinnamon

250 g/9 oz long-grain rice

425 ml/15 fl oz natural yogurt

60 g/2¼ oz sultanas

200 ml/7 fl oz chicken stock

1 tomato, chopped

2 tbsp chopped fresh coriander or parsley

2 tbsp coconut, toasted

salt and pepper

fresh coriander, to garnish

1 Heat the butter in a heavy or non-stick pan and fry the chicken with the onion for about 3 minutes.

2 Stir in the turmeric, cinnamon, rice and seasoning and fry gently for 3 minutes.

3 Add the natural yogurt, sultanas and chicken stock and mix well. Cover and simmer for 10 minutes, stirring occasionally until the rice is tender and all the chicken stock has been absorbed. Add more stock if the mixture starts to become too dry.

4 Stir in the chopped tomato and fresh coriander or parsley. Season to taste.

5 Sprinkle the Golden Chicken Pilau with the toasted coconut and garnish with fresh coriander.

COOK'S TIP

Long-grain rice is the most widely available and the cheapest rice. Basmati, with its slender grains and aromatic flavour, is more expensive. All rice, especially basmati, should be washed thoroughly under cold, running water before use.

Chicken & Chinese Leaves

The great thing about stir-fries is you can cook with very little fat and still get lots of flavour, as in this light, healthy lunch dish.

NUTRITIONAL INFORMATION

Calories 329	Sugars 3g
Protein 25g	Fat 4g
Carbohydrate ...46g	Saturates 1g

 15 mins   25 mins

SERVES 4

INGREDIENTS

200 g/7 oz rice stick noodles

1 tbsp sunflower oil

1 garlic clove, finely chopped

2 cm/¾ inch piece fresh root ginger, finely chopped

4 spring onions, chopped

1 red bird-eye chilli, deseeded and sliced

300 g/10½ oz boneless, skinless chicken, finely chopped

2 chicken livers, finely chopped

1 celery stick, thinly sliced

1 carrot, cut into fine matchsticks

300 g/10½ oz shredded Chinese leaves

4 tbsp lime juice

2 tbsp Thai fish sauce

1 tbsp soy sauce

TO GARNISH

2 tbsp fresh mint, shredded

slices of pickled garlic

fresh mint sprig

1 Soak the rice noodles in hot water for 15 minutes, or according to the package directions. Drain well.

2 Heat the oil in a wok or large frying pan and stir-fry the garlic, ginger, spring onions and chilli for about 1 minute. Stir in the chicken and chicken livers, then stir-fry over a high heat for 2–3 minutes, or until beginning to brown.

3 Stir in the celery and carrot and stir-fry for 2 minutes to soften. Add the Chinese leaves, then stir in the lime juice, fish sauce and soy sauce.

4 Add the noodles and stir to heat thoroughly. Sprinkle with shredded mint and pickled garlic. Serve immediately, garnished with a mint sprig.

Chicken Tacos from Puebla

Seasoned chicken fills these soft tacos, along with creamy refried beans, avocado, smoky chipotle and soured cream. It is a feast of tastes.

NUTRITIONAL INFORMATION

Calories	674	Sugars	.........6g
Protein	........34g	Fat	..........25g
Carbohydrate	...80g	Saturates	.......9g

 10 mins   5 mins

SERVES 4

I N G R E D I E N T S

8 corn tortillas

2 tsp vegetable oil

225–350 g/8–12 oz leftover cooked chicken, diced or shredded

225 g/8 oz can refried beans, warmed with 2 tbsp water to thin

¼ tsp ground cumin

¼ tsp dried oregano

1 avocado, stoned, sliced and tossed with lime juice

salsa verde or salsa of your choice

1 canned chipotle chilli in adobo marinade, chopped, or bottled chipotle salsa

175 ml/6 fl oz soured cream

½ onion, chopped

handful of lettuce leaves

5 radishes, diced

salt and pepper

1 Heat the tortillas for a few seconds each in an ungreased non-stick frying pan in a stack, alternating the top and bottom tortillas so that the tortillas heat evenly. Wrap in kitchen foil or a clean tea towel to keep warm.

2 Heat the oil in a frying pan, add the diced or shredded chicken and heat through. Season with salt and pepper according to taste.

3 Thoroughly combine the refried beans with the cumin and oregano.

4 Spread one tortilla with warm refried beans, then top with a spoonful of the chicken, a slice or two of avocado, a dab of salsa, chipotle to taste, a dollop of soured cream and a sprinkling of onion, lettuce and radishes. Season with salt and pepper according to taste, then roll up, as tightly as you can. Repeat with the remaining tortillas and serve at once.

VARIATION

Replace the chicken with 450 g/1 lb minced beef browned with a seasoning of chopped onion, mild chilli powder and ground cumin to taste.

Green Chilli Chilaquiles

Easy to put together, this dish makes a perfect mid-week supper. Use tortilla chips instead of baking the tortillas, if you prefer.

NUTRITIONAL INFORMATION

Calories 682   Sugars 1g
Protein ....60g   Fat 38g
Carbohydrate ...26g   Saturates 20g

 15 mins   1 hr

SERVES 4–6

I N G R E D I E N T S

12 stale tortillas, cut into strips

1 tbsp vegetable oil

1 small cooked chicken, meat removed from the bones and cut into bite-sized pieces

salsa verde

3 tbsp chopped fresh coriander

1 tsp finely chopped fresh oregano or thyme

4 garlic cloves, finely chopped

¼ tsp ground cumin

350 g/12 oz grated cheese, such as Cheddar, manchego or mozzarella

450 ml/16 fl oz chicken stock

115 g/4 oz Parmesan cheese, freshly grated

TO SERVE

350 ml/12 fl oz crème fraîche or soured cream

3–5 spring onions, thinly sliced

pickled chillies

1 Place the tortilla strips in a roasting tin, toss with oil and bake in a preheated oven, 190°C/375°F/Gas Mark 5, for 30 minutes, or until they are crisp and golden.

2 Arrange the chicken in a 23 x 33 cm/9 x 13 inch casserole, then sprinkle with half the salsa, coriander, oregano, garlic, cumin and some of the cheese. Repeat these layers and top with the tortilla strips.

3 Pour the stock over the top, then sprinkle with the remaining cheeses.

4 Bake in a preheated oven at 190°C/375°F/Gas Mark 5 for about 30 minutes, or until heated through and the cheese is lightly golden in areas.

5 Serve garnished with the crème fraîche, sliced spring onions and pickled chillies to taste.

Potato & Banana Cakes

Potato cakes are usually served plain on the side. Here, they are combined with minced chicken and mashed banana for a fruit-flavoured main course.

NUTRITIONAL INFORMATION

Calories 429	Sugars 11g	
Protein 22g	Fat 23g	
Carbohydrate ...39g	Saturates 10g	

15 mins   30 mins

SERVES 4

INGREDIENTS

450 g/1 lb floury potatoes, diced

225 g/8 oz minced chicken

1 large banana

2 tbsp plain flour

1 tsp lemon juice

1 onion, finely chopped

2 tbsp chopped fresh sage

2 tbsp butter

2 tbsp vegetable oil

150 ml/5 fl oz single cream

150 ml/5 fl oz chicken stock

salt and pepper

fresh sage leaves, to garnish

1 Cook the potatoes in boiling water for 10 minutes. Drain and mash the potatoes until smooth. Stir in the chicken.

2 Mash the banana and add it to the potato with the flour, lemon juice, onion and half the chopped sage. Season well and stir the mixture together.

3 Divide the mixture into 8 equal portions. With lightly floured hands, shape each portion into a round patty.

4 Heat butter and oil in a frying pan, add the patties and cook for 12–15 minutes, turning once. Remove and keep warm.

5 Stir the cream and stock into the pan with the remaining chopped sage. Cook over a low heat for 2–3 minutes.

6 Arrange the potato cakes on a serving plate, garnish with fresh sage leaves and serve with the cream and sage sauce.

COOK'S TIP
Do not boil the sauce once the cream has been added as it will curdle. Cook it gently over a very low heat.

Golden Chicken Risotto

Only risotto rice will give this dish the creamy succulence everyone expects of the classic Italian risotto.

NUTRITIONAL INFORMATION

Calories 701	Sugars 7g
Protein 35g	Fat 26g
Carbohydrate . . .88g	Saturates 8g

 10 mins   30 mins

SERVES 4

INGREDIENTS

2 tbsp sunflower oil

1 tbsp butter or margarine

1 leek, thinly sliced

1 large yellow pepper, diced

3 skinless, boneless chicken breasts, diced

350 g/12 oz arborio rice

strands of saffron

1.5 litres/2¾ pints chicken stock

200 g/7 oz can sweetcorn

60 g/2¼ oz unsalted peanuts, toasted

60 g/2¼ oz Parmesan cheese, grated

salt and pepper

1 Heat oil and butter in a saucepan. Fry the leek and pepper for 1 minute, stir in the chicken and cook, stirring, until golden.

2 Stir in the arborio rice and cook for 2–3 minutes.

3 Stir in the saffron strands and salt and pepper. Add the chicken stock, a little at a time, cover and cook over a low heat, stirring occasionally, for about 20 minutes, or until the rice is tender and most of the liquid has been absorbed. Do not let the risotto dry out – add more stock if necessary.

4 Stir in the sweetcorn, peanuts and freshly-grated Parmesan cheese, then season with salt and pepper according to taste. Serve piping hot.

COOK'S TIP

Risottos can be frozen, before adding the Parmesan cheese, for up to 1 month, but remember to reheat this risotto thoroughly as it contains chicken.

Steamed Chicken Parcels

A healthy recipe with a delicate oriental flavour. Use large spinach leaves to wrap around the chicken, but make sure they are young leaves.

NUTRITIONAL INFORMATION

Calories 216	Sugars 7g
Protein 31g	Fat 7g
Carbohydrate 7g	Saturates 2g

5 mins   30 mins

SERVES 4

I N G R E D I E N T S

4 lean boneless, skinless chicken breasts

1 tsp ground lemon grass

2 spring onions, chopped finely

250 g/9 oz young carrots

250 g/9 oz young courgettes

2 celery sticks

1 tsp light soy sauce

250 g/9 oz spinach leaves

2 tsp sesame oil

salt and pepper

1 With a sharp knife, make a slit through one side of each chicken breast, to open out a large pocket.

2 Sprinkle the inside of the pocket with lemon grass, salt and pepper. Tuck the spring onions into each of the chicken pockets.

3 Trim the carrots, courgettes and celery, then cut into small match-sticks. Plunge them into a pan of boiling water for 1 minute, then drain and toss in the soy sauce.

4 Pack the mixture into the pockets in each chicken breast and fold over firmly to enclose. Reserve the remaining vegetables. Wash and dry the spinach leaves, then wrap the chicken breasts firmly in the leaves to enclose completely. If the leaves are too firm, steam them for a few seconds until they are softened and flexible.

5 Place the wrapped chicken in a steamer and steam over rapidly boiling water for 20–25 minutes, depending on size.

6 Stir-fry any leftover vegetable sticks and spinach for 1–2 minutes in the sesame oil and serve with the chicken.

Chicken with Cashew Nuts

This is a well-known dish, popular in Chinese restaurants throughout the West. It can taste even better if you make it yourself.

NUTRITIONAL INFORMATION

Calories 330	Sugars 5g	
Protein 22g	Fat 18g	
Carbohydrate ...19g	Saturates 3g	

10 mins, plus 20 mins to marinate   15 mins

SERVES 4

INGREDIENTS

300 g/10½ oz boneless, skinless chicken breasts

1 tbsp cornflour

1 tsp sesame oil

1 tbsp hoisin sauce

1 tsp light soy sauce

3 garlic cloves, crushed

2 tbsp vegetable oil

75 g/2¾ oz unsalted cashew nuts

25 g/1 oz mangetouts

1 celery stick, sliced

1 onion, cut into 8 pieces

60 g/2¼ oz beansprouts

1 red pepper, deseeded and diced

SAUCE

2 tsp cornflour

2 tbsp hoisin sauce

200 ml/7 fl oz chicken stock

1 Trim any fat from the chicken breasts and cut the meat into thin strips. Place the chicken in a large mixing bowl. Sprinkle with the cornflour and toss to coat the chicken strips in it, shaking off any excess. Mix together the sesame oil, hoisin sauce, soy sauce and 1 garlic clove. Pour this mixture over the chicken, turning to coat thoroughly. Leave to marinate for 20 minutes.

2 Heat half of the vegetable oil in a preheated wok. Add the cashew nuts and stir-fry for 1 minute, or until browned. Add the mangetouts, celery, the remaining garlic, the onion, beansprouts and red pepper and cook, stirring occasionally, for 2–3 minutes. Remove the vegetables from the wok with a slotted spoon, set aside and keep warm.

3 Heat the remaining oil in the wok. Remove the chicken from the marinade and stir-fry for 3–4 minutes. Return the vegetables to the wok.

4 To make the sauce, mix the cornflour, hoisin sauce and chicken stock together and pour into the wok. Bring to the boil, stirring until thickened and clear. Serve immediately on warm serving plates.

Chicken Fu Yung

Although commonly described as an omelette, fu yung ('white lotus petals') should use only egg whites to create a very delicate texture.

NUTRITIONAL INFORMATION

Calories 220	Sugars 1g
Protein 16g	Fat 14g
Carbohydrate 7g	Saturates 3g

 10 mins   5 mins

SERVES 4

I N G R E D I E N T S

175 g/6 oz chicken breast fillet, skinned

½ tsp salt

pepper

1 tsp rice wine or dry sherry

1 tbsp cornflour

3 eggs

salt

½ tsp spring onions, finely chopped

3 tbsp vegetable oil

125 g/4¼ oz green peas

1 tsp light soy sauce

drops of sesame oil

1 Cut the chicken across the grain into very small, paper-thin slices, using a cleaver. Place the chicken slices in a shallow dish.

2 In a small bowl, mix together ½ teaspoon salt, pepper, rice wine or dry sherry and cornflour.

3 Pour the mixture over the chicken slices in the dish, turning the chicken until well coated.

4 Beat the eggs in a small bowl with a pinch of salt and the spring onions.

5 Heat the vegetable oil in a preheated wok, add the chicken slices and stir-fry for about 1 minute, making sure that the slices are kept separated.

6 Pour the beaten eggs over the chicken, and lightly scramble until set. Do not stir too vigorously, or the mixture will break up in the oil. Stir the oil from the bottom of the wok so that the fu-yung rises to the surface.

7 Add the peas, light soy sauce and salt to taste and blend well. Transfer the fu yung to warm serving dishes, sprinkle it with sesame oil, and serve.

COOK'S TIP
If available, chicken goujons can be used for this dish: these are small, delicate strips of chicken which require no further cutting and are very tender.

Chicken Noodles

Rice noodles are a main ingredient in this delicious recipe. Buy them fromlarge supermarkets or specialist oriental stores.

NUTRITIONAL INFORMATION

Calories	169	Sugars	.........2g
Protein	........14g	Fat	...........7g
Carbohydrate	...12g	Saturates	.......2g

 5 mins 15 mins

SERVES 4

INGREDIENTS

225 g/8 oz rice noodles

2 tbsp peanut oil

225 g/8 oz skinless, boneless chicken breast, sliced

2 garlic cloves, crushed

1 tsp grated fresh root ginger

1 tsp Chinese curry powder

1 red pepper, deseeded and thinly sliced

75 g/2¾ oz mangetouts, shredded

1 tbsp light soy sauce

2 tsp Chinese rice wine

2 tbsp chicken stock

1 tsp sesame oil

1 tbsp chopped fresh coriander

VARIATION

For a tasty change, use pork or duck in this recipe instead of chicken.

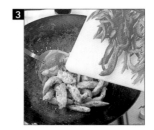

1 Soak the rice noodles for 4 minutes in warm water. Drain thoroughly and set aside until required.

2 Heat the peanut oil in a preheated wok or large heavy-based frying pan and stir-fry the chicken slices for 2–3 minutes.

3 Add the garlic, ginger and Chinese curry powder and stir-fry for a further 30 seconds. Add the red pepper and mangetouts to the mixture in the wok and stir-fry for 2–3 minutes.

4 Add the noodles, soy sauce, Chinese rice wine and chicken stock to the wok and mix well, stirring occasionally, for 1 minute.

5 Sprinkle the sesame oil and chopped coriander over the noodles. Transfer to serving plates and serve.

Chicken & Cheese Jackets

Use the breasts from a roasted chicken to make these delicious potatoes, and serve them as a light lunch or supper dish.

NUTRITIONAL INFORMATION

Calories	417	Sugars	........4g
Protein	........28g	Fat	..........10g
Carbohydrate	...57g	Saturates	......5g

 5 mins   50 mins

SERVES 4

INGREDIENTS

4 large baking potatoes

225 g/8 oz cooked, boneless
  chicken breasts

4 spring onions

250 g/9 oz low-fat soft cheese
  or Quark

pepper

1 Scrub the baking potatoes and pat them dry thoroughly with absorbent kitchen paper.

2 Prick the potatoes all over with a fork. Bake in a preheated oven, 200°C/400°F/Gas Mark 6, for about 50 minutes until tender, or cook in a microwave on a high setting for 12–15 minutes.

3 Using a sharp knife, dice the chicken and trim and thickly slice the spring onions. Place the chicken and spring onions in a bowl.

4 Add the low-fat soft cheese or Quark to the chicken and spring onions and stir well to combine.

5 Cut a cross through the top of each potato and pull slightly apart. Spoon the chicken filling into the potatoes and sprinkle with pepper.

6 Serve the chicken and cheese jackets immediately with coleslaw, green salad or a mixed salad.

COOK'S TIP
Look for Quark in the chiller cabinet of your local store. It is a low-fat, white, fresh curd cheese made from cow's milk. It has a delicate, slightly sour flavour.

Chicken Jalfrezi

This is a quick and tasty way to use leftover roast chicken. The sauce can also be used for any cooked poultry, lamb or beef.

NUTRITIONAL INFORMATION

Calories	.270	Sugars	.3g
Protein	.36g	Fat	.11g
Carbohydrate	.7g	Saturates	.2g

 15 mins 15 mins

SERVES 4

INGREDIENTS

1 tsp mustard oil

3 tbsp vegetable oil

1 large onion, chopped finely

3 garlic cloves, crushed

1 tbsp tomato purée

2 tomatoes, skinned and chopped

1 tsp ground turmeric

½ tsp cumin seeds, ground

½ tsp coriander seeds, ground

½ tsp chilli powder

½ tsp garam masala

1 tsp red wine vinegar

1 small red pepper, chopped

125 g/4¼ oz frozen broad beans

500 g/1 lb 2 oz cooked chicken, cut into bite-sized pieces

salt

sprigs of fresh coriander, to garnish

1 Heat the mustard oil in a large, frying pan set over a high heat for approximately 1 minute, or until the oil begins to smoke.

2 Add the vegetable oil, reduce the heat and then add the onion and the garlic. Fry the garlic and onion until they are golden.

3 Add the tomato purée, chopped tomatoes, turmeric, ground cumin and coriander seeds, chilli powder, garam masala and wine vinegar to the frying pan. Stir the mixture until fragrant.

4 Add the red pepper and broad beans and stir for 2 minutes, or until the pepper is softened. Stir in the chicken, and salt to taste.

5 Simmer gently for 6–8 minutes, or until the chicken is heated through and the beans are tender.

6 Serve as soon after cooking as possible, garnished with sprigs of fresh coriander.

Oriental Chicken Salad

Mirin (the Japanese sweet rice wine), soy sauce and sesame oil give an oriental flavour to this delicious salad.

NUTRITIONAL INFORMATION

Calories	361	Sugars	.........2g
Protein	........34g	Fat	..........16g
Carbohydrate	...17g	Saturates	.......3g

 10 mins   35 mins

SERVES 4

INGREDIENTS

4 skinless, boneless chicken breasts

75 ml/2½ fl oz mirin or sweet sherry

75 ml/2½ fl oz light soy sauce

1 tbsp sesame oil

3 tbsp olive oil

1 tbsp red wine vinegar

1 tbsp Dijon mustard

250 g/9 oz egg noodles

250 g/9 oz bean sprouts

250 g/9 oz Chinese leaves, shredded

2 spring onions, sliced

125 g/4¼ oz mushrooms, sliced

1 fresh red chilli, finely sliced,
  to garnish

1 Pound the boneless chicken breasts out to an even thickness between two sheets of cling film with a rolling pin or cleaver.

2 Put the chicken breasts in a roasting tin. Combine the mirin and soy sauce and brush over the chicken.

3 Place the chicken in a preheated oven, 200°C/400°F/Gas Mark 6, for 20–30 minutes, basting often.

4 Remove the chicken from the oven and allow to cool slightly.

5 Combine the sesame oil, olive oil and red wine vinegar with the mustard.

6 Cook the noodles according to the instructions on the packet. Rinse under cold running water, then drain.

7 Toss the noodles in the dressing until the noodles are completely coated.

8 Toss the bean sprouts, Chinese leaves, spring onions and mushrooms together with the noodles.

9 Slice the cooked chicken very thinly and stir into the noodles. Garnish the salad with the chilli slices and serve.

Chicken Pan Bagna

Perfect for a picnic or packed lunch, this Mediterranean-style sandwich can be prepared in very little time, and well ahead of its serving time.

NUTRITIONAL INFORMATION

Calories	366	Sugars	.........2g
Protein	........20g	Fat	..........23g
Carbohydrate	...20g	Saturates	.......4g

 5 mins   0 mins

SERVES 6

I N G R E D I E N T S

1 large French stick

1 garlic clove

125 ml/4 fl oz good quality olive oil

20 g/¾ oz canned anchovy fillets

50 g/1¾ oz cold roast chicken

2 large tomatoes, sliced

8 large, pitted black olives, chopped

pepper

1 Using a sharp bread knife, cut the French stick in half lengthways and open it out flat.

2 Cut the garlic clove in half and rub it liberally over the bread.

3 Sprinkle the cut surface of the garlic-flavoured bread lightly with the olive oil, and let the flavourings soak in.

4 Drain the canned anchovies and set aside temporarily.

5 Thinly slice the chicken and arrange on top of the bread. Arrange the tomatoes and anchovies on top of the chicken.

6 Scatter with the olives and pepper. Sandwich the loaf back together and wrap in foil before serving in slices.

VARIATION

Use Italian ciabatta or olive-studded focaccia bread instead of the French stick.

Coronation Chicken

This classic salad is good as a starter or as part of a buffet. Mango chutney makes a tasty accompaniment.

NUTRITIONAL INFORMATION	
Calories 660	Sugars 5g
Protein 40g	Fat 53g
Carbohydrate 7g	Saturates 9g

 10 mins   15 mins

SERVES 6

I N G R E D I E N T S

4 tbsp olive oil

900 g/2 lb chicken, diced

125 g/4¼ oz rindless, smoked bacon, diced

12 shallots

2 garlic cloves, crushed

1 tbsp mild curry powder

300 ml/10 fl oz mayonnaise

1 tbsp runny honey

1 tbsp chopped fresh parsley

pepper

90 g/3¼ oz seedless black grapes, quartered

cold saffron rice, to serve

1 Heat the oil in a large frying pan and add the chicken, bacon, shallots, garlic and curry powder. Cook slowly for about 15 minutes.

2 Spoon the cooked mixture into a clean mixing bowl.

3 Allow the mixture to cool completely before seasoning it with pepper according to taste.

4 Blend the mayonnaise with a little honey, then add the chopped fresh parsley. Toss the chicken in the mixture.

5 Place the mixture in a deep serving dish, garnish with the grapes and serve with cold saffron rice.

VARIATION
Add 2 tbsp chopped fresh apricots and 2 tbsp flaked almonds to the sauce in Step 4.

Indonesian Chicken Salad

The spicy peanut dressing served with this salad may be prepared in advance and left to chill a day before required.

NUTRITIONAL INFORMATION

Calories 802	Sugars 15g
Protein 35g	Fat 55g
Carbohydrate . . .45g	Saturates 10g

 15 mins   10 mins

SERVES 4

INGREDIENTS

4 large waxy potatoes, diced

300 g/10½ oz fresh pineapple, diced

2 carrots, grated

175 g/6 oz beansprouts

1 bunch spring onions, sliced

1 large courgette, cut into matchsticks

3 celery sticks, cut into matchsticks

175 g/6 oz unsalted peanuts

2 cooked chicken breast fillets (about 125 g/4¼ oz each), sliced

DRESSING

6 tbsp crunchy peanut butter

6 tbsp olive oil

2 tbsp light soy sauce

1 red chilli, chopped

2 tsp sesame oil

4 tsp lime juice

COOK'S TIP

Unsweetened canned pineapple may be used in place of the fresh pineapple for convenience. If only sweetened, canned pineapple is available, drain it and rinse under cold running water before using.

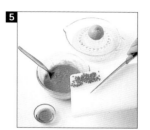

1 Cook the diced potatoes in a saucepan of boiling water for 10 minutes or until tender. Drain and leave to cool.

2 Transfer the cooled potatoes to a salad bowl.

3 Add the pineapple, carrots, beansprouts, spring onions, courgette, celery, peanuts and sliced chicken to the potatoes. Toss well to mix.

4 To make the dressing, put the peanut butter in a small bowl and gradually whisk in the olive oil and light soy sauce.

5 Stir in the chopped red chilli, sesame oil and lime juice. Mix well.

6 Pour the spicy dressing over the salad and toss lightly to coat all of the ingredients. Serve the salad immediately, garnished with the lime wedges.

Spicy Chicken Salad

Tender chicken breast meat cut into small pieces is perfect for salads. The chicken pieces cook quickly and can be tossed with other salad ingredients.

NUTRITIONAL INFORMATION

Calories 259	Sugars 9g	
Protein 18g	Fat 12g	
Carbohydrate ...22g	Saturates 5g	

10 mins   25 mins

SERVES 4

I N G R E D I E N T S

2 skinned chicken breast fillets (about 125 g/4¼ oz each)

2 tbsp butter

1 red chilli, chopped

1 tbsp clear honey

½ tsp ground cumin

2 tbsp chopped fresh coriander

2 large potatoes, diced

50 g/1¾ oz thin green beans, halved

1 red pepper, cut into thin strips

2 tomatoes, deseeded and diced

D R E S S I N G

2 tbsp olive oil

pinch of chilli powder

1 tbsp garlic wine vinegar

pinch of caster sugar

1 tbsp chopped fresh coriander

1 Cut the chicken breast fillets into thin strips using a sharp knife. Melt the butter in a medium-sized saucepan over a medium heat and then add the chicken, chilli, honey and cumin. Cook together for approximately 10 minutes, turning until cooked through.

2 Transfer to a clean bowl, leave to cool, then stir in the coriander.

3 Meanwhile, cook the diced potatoes in a saucepan of boiling water for 10 minutes, or until tender. Drain and leave to cool.

4 Blanch the green beans in a saucepan full of boiling water for 3 minutes. Drain them thoroughly and set aside to cool. Mix the green beans and potatoes together in a salad bowl.

5 Add the pepper strips and diced tomatoes to the potatoes and beans. Stir in the spicy chicken mixture.

6 In a small bowl, whisk the dressing ingredients together and pour the dressing over the salad, tossing well. Serve at once.

Pasta & Chicken Medley

Strips of cooked chicken are tossed with coloured pasta, grapes and carrot sticks in a Mediterranean-style pesto-flavoured dressing.

NUTRITIONAL INFORMATION

Calories	609	Sugars	........11g
Protein	........26g	Fat	..........38g
Carbohydrate	...45g	Saturates	.......6g

 20 mins   10 mins

SERVES 2

FRENCH DRESSING

1 tbsp wine vinegar

3 tbsp extra-virgin olive oil

salt and pepper

INGREDIENTS

125–150 g/4¼–5½ oz dried pasta shapes, such as twists or bows

1 tbsp oil

2 tbsp mayonnaise

2 tsp bottled pesto sauce

1 tbsp soured cream or natural fromage frais

175 g/6 oz cooked skinless, boneless chicken

1–2 celery sticks

125 g/4½ oz black grapes (preferably seedless)

1 large carrot, trimmed

salt and pepper

celery leaves, to garnish

1 To make the dressing, whisk all the ingredients until evenly blended.

2 Cook the pasta with the oil for 8–10 minutes in boiling, salted water. Drain, rinse, drain again, transfer to a bowl and mix in 1 tablespoon of dressing; set aside.

3 Combine the mayonnaise, pesto sauce and soured cream or fromage frais in a clean bowl, and season with salt and pepper according to taste.

4 Cut the chicken into narrow strips. Cut the celery diagonally into narrow slices. Reserve a few grapes for garnish, halve the rest and remove any pips. Cut the carrot into narrow julienne strips.

5 Add the chicken, the celery, the halved grapes, the carrot and the mayonnaise mixture to the cool pasta, and toss thoroughly. Check the seasoning, adding more salt and pepper if necessary.

6 Arrange the pasta mixture on two plates. Garnish with the reserved black grapes and the celery leaves and serve immediately.

Chargrilled Chicken Salad

This is a quick starter to serve at a barbecue. If the bread is folded in half, the chicken salad can be put in the middle and eaten as finger food.

NUTRITIONAL INFORMATION

Calories 225   Sugars 5g
Protein . . . . .16g   Fat 12g
Carbohydrate . . .15g   Saturates 2g

    10 mins   15 mins

SERVES 4

INGREDIENTS

2 skinless, boneless chicken breasts

1 red onion

oil for brushing

1 avocado, peeled and pitted

1 tbsp lemon juice

125 ml/4 fl oz low-fat mayonnaise

¼ tsp chilli powder

½ tsp pepper

¼ tsp salt

4 tomatoes, quartered

½ loaf sun-dried tomato-flavoured focaccia bread

green salad, to serve

1 Using a sharp knife, cut the chicken breasts into 1 cm/½ inch strips.

2 Cut the onion into eight pieces, held together at the root. Rinse under cold running water and then brush with oil.

3 Purée or mash the avocado and lemon juice together. Whisk in the mayonnaise. Add the chilli powder, pepper and salt.

4 Put the chicken and onion over a hot barbecue and grill for 3–4 minutes on

each side. Combine the chicken, onion, tomatoes and avocado mixture together.

5 Cut the bread in half twice, so that you have quarter-circle shaped pieces, then in half horizontally. Toast on the hot barbecue for about 2 minutes on each side.

6 Spoon the chicken mixture on to the toasts and serve with a green salad.

VARIATION

Instead of focaccia, serve the salad in pitta breads which have been warmed through on the barbecue.

Spinach Salad

Fresh baby spinach is tasty and light, and it makes an excellent salad to go with the chicken and the creamy, orange-flavoured dressing.

NUTRITIONAL INFORMATION

Calories 145	Sugars 3g	
Protein 10g	Fat 10g	
Carbohydrate 4g	Saturates 1g	

🍲 15 mins 🕐 0 mins

SERVES 4

INGREDIENTS

50 g/1¾ oz mushrooms

100 g/3½ oz baby spinach, washed

75 g/2¾ oz radicchio leaves, shredded

100 g/3½ oz cooked chicken breast

50 g/1¾ oz Parma ham

DRESSING

2 tbsp olive oil

½ orange, finely grated rind, and 1 orange, juiced

1 tbsp natural yogurt

1 Wipe the mushrooms with a damp cloth to remove any excess dirt.

2 Gently mix together the spinach and radicchio in a large salad bowl.

3 Using a sharp knife, thinly slice the wiped mushrooms and add them to the bowl containing the baby spinach and radicchio leaves, ready for the addition of the other salad ingredients.

4 Tear the cooked chicken breast and Parma ham into strips with the your hands and mix them thoroughly into the spinach salad.

5 To make the dressing, place the olive oil, orange rind, juice and yogurt into a screw-top jar. Shake the jar until the mixture is well combined. Season to taste with salt and pepper.

6 Drizzle the yogurt and orange dressing over the spinach salad and toss to mix it in well well. Serve in the bowl or on individual plates.

VARIATION

Spinach is delicious when served raw. Try raw spinach in a salad garnished with bacon or garlicky croûtons. The young leaves have a wonderfully sharp flavour.

Chinese Chicken Salad

This is a refreshing dish suitable for a summer meal or a light lunch. It is a healthy dish, composed of fresh vegetables and low in fat.

NUTRITIONAL INFORMATION

Calories	162	Sugars	.........3g
Protein	.........15g	Fat	...........10g
Carbohydrate	....5g	Saturates	.......2g

20 mins, plus 20 mins to marinate   10 mins

SERVES 4

I N G R E D I E N T S

225 g/8 oz skinless, boneless chicken breasts

2 tsp light soy sauce

1 tsp sesame oil

1 tsp sesame seeds

2 tbsp vegetable oil

125 g/4¼ oz bean sprouts

1 red pepper, deseeded and thinly sliced

1 carrot, cut into matchsticks

3 baby corn cobs, sliced

snipped chives and carrot matchsticks, to garnish

S A U C E

2 tsp rice wine vinegar

1 tbsp light soy sauce

dash of chilli oil

1 Place the chicken breasts in a shallow glass dish.

2 Mix the soy sauce and sesame oil and pour over the chicken. Sprinkle with sesame seeds and leave for 20 minutes, turning the chicken over occasionally.

3 Remove the chicken from the marinade and cut the meat into thin slices using a sharp knife.

4 Heat the vegetable oil in a preheated wok or large frying pan. Add the chicken and fry for 4–5 minutes, or until cooked through and golden brown on both sides. Remove the chicken from the wok with a slotted spoon, set aside and leave to cool.

5 Add the bean sprouts, pepper, carrot and baby corn cobs to the wok and stir-fry for 2–3 minutes. Remove from the wok with a slotted spoon, set aside and leave to cool.

6 For the sauce, mix the rice wine vinegar, light soy sauce and chilli oil.

7 Arrange the chicken and vegetables on a serving plate. Spoon over the sauce and garnish with chives and carrots.

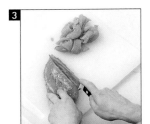

Layered Chicken Salad

This layered main-course salad has lively tastes and textures. For an interesting variation, substitute canned tuna for the chicken.

NUTRITIONAL INFORMATION

Calories 352	Sugars 9g
Protein 29g	Fat 9g
Carbohydrate . . .43g	Saturates 2g

 20 mins 40 mins

SERVES 4

INGREDIENTS

750 g/1 lb 10 oz new potatoes, scrubbed

1 red pepper, halved, cored and deseeded

1 green pepper, halved, cored and deseeded

2 small courgettes, sliced

1 small onion, thinly sliced

3 tomatoes, sliced

350 g/12 oz cooked chicken, sliced

snipped fresh chives, to garnish

YOGURT DRESSING

150 g/5½ oz low-fat natural yogurt

3 tbsp low-fat mayonnaise

1 tbsp snipped fresh chives

salt and pepper

1 Place the new potatoes in a large saucepan pan of cold water. Bring to the boil, then reduce the heat. Cover and simmer for 15–20 minutes until tender.

2 Meanwhile place the pepper halves, cut side down, under a preheated hot grill and grill until the skins blacken and begin to char.

3 Remove the peppers and leave to cool, then peel off the skins and slice the flesh. Set to one side.

4 Cook the courgettes in a small amount of lightly salted boiling water for 3 minutes.

5 Rinse the courgettes with cold water to cool quickly and set aside.

6 To make the dressing, mix the yogurt, mayonnaise, and snipped chives together in a small bowl. Season well with salt and pepper.

7 Drain, cool and slice the potatoes. Add them to the dressing and mix well to coat evenly. Divide between 4 individual serving plates.

8 Top each plate with one quarter of the pepper slices and cooked courgettes. Layer one quarter of the onion and tomato slices, then the sliced chicken, on top of each serving. Garnish with snipped fresh chives and serve.

Chicken & Grape Salad

Tender chicken breast, sweet grapes and crisp celery coated in a mild curry mayonnaise make a wonderful al fresco lunch.

NUTRITIONAL INFORMATION

Calories	413	Sugars	. . . . .20g
Protein	. . . . .39g	Fat	. . . . .20g
Carbohydrate	. . .20g	Saturates	. . . . . .3g

  15 mins 0 mins

SERVES 4

INGREDIENTS

500 g/1 lb 2 oz cooked skinless, boneless chicken breasts

2 celery sticks, sliced finely

250 g/9 oz black grapes

60 g/2¼ oz split almonds, toasted

pinch of paprika

sprigs of fresh coriander or flat-leaved parsley, to garnish

CURRY SAUCE

150 ml/5 fl oz low-fat mayonnaise

125 g/4¼ oz natural low-fat fromage frais

1 tbsp clear honey

1 tbsp curry paste

1 Cut the chicken into fairly large pieces and transfer to a bowl with the sliced celery.

2 Halve the grapes, remove the seeds, and add to the bowl.

3 To make the curry sauce, mix the mayonnaise, fromage frais, honey and curry paste carefully together until they are well blended.

4 Pour the curry sauce over the salad and mix together carefully until chicken and grapes are thoroughly coated.

5 Transfer to a shallow serving dish and sprinkle with the split almonds and paprika.

6 Serve in the bowl or on individual plates. garnished with sprigs or coriander or flat-leaved parsley.

COOK'S TIP

To save time, use seedless grapes, now widely available in supermarkets, and add them whole to the salad.

Waldorf Chicken Salad

This colourful and healthy dish is a variation of a classic salad. You can use a selection of mixed salad leaves, if preferred.

NUTRITIONAL INFORMATION

Calories	471	Sugars	....19g
Protein	....38g	Fat	....27g
Carbohydrate	...20g	Saturates	....4g

15 mins, plus 40 mins to marinate 45 mins

SERVES 4

INGREDIENTS

500 g/1 lb 2 oz red apples, diced

3 tbsp fresh lemon juice

150 ml/5 fl oz low-fat mayonnaise

1 head of celery

4 shallots, sliced

1 garlic clove, crushed

90 g/3¼ oz walnuts, chopped

500 g/1 lb 2 oz lean cooked chicken, cubed

1 cos lettuce

pepper

sliced apple and walnuts, to garnish

VARIATION
Instead of the shallots, use spring onions for a milder flavour. Trim the spring onions and slice finely.

1 Place the apples in a bowl with the lemon juice and 1 tablespoon of mayonnaise. Leave for at least 40 minutes, or until required.

2 Slice the head of celery very thinly. Add the celery together with the shallots, garlic and walnuts to the coated apples, mix them well and then add the remaining mayonnaise before blending thoroughly.

3 Add the chicken and mix with the other ingredients.

4 Line a glass salad bowl or serving dish with the lettuce.

5 Pile the chicken salad into the centre, sprinkle with pepper and garnish with apple slices and walnuts.

Old English Spicy Salad

This is an excellent recipe for leftover roast chicken. Add the dressing just before serving, so that the spinach retains its crispness.

NUTRITIONAL INFORMATION

Calories ....225 Sugars 4g
Protein ....25g Fat 12g
Carbohydrate ....4g Saturates 2g

 10 mins   0 mins

SERVES 4

INGREDIENTS

225 g/8 oz young spinach leaves

3 celery sticks, sliced thinly

½ cucumber, sliced thinly

2 spring onions, sliced thinly

3 tbsp chopped fresh parsley

350g/12 oz boneless, lean roast chicken, sliced thinly

DRESSING

2.5 cm/1 inch piece fresh root ginger, grated finely

3 tbsp olive oil

1 tbsp white wine vinegar

1 tbsp clear honey

½ tsp ground cinnamon

salt and pepper

smoked almonds, to garnish (optional)

  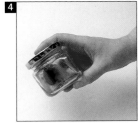

1 Thoroughly wash and dry the young spinach leaves.

2 Toss the celery, cucumber and spring onions with the spinach and parsley in a large bowl.

3 Transfer the salad ingredients to serving plates and arrange the chicken over the salad.

4 To make the dressing, combine the grated ginger, olive oil, wine vinegar, honey and cinnamon in a screw-topped jar and shake well to mix. Season with salt and pepper to taste.

5 Pour the dressing over the salad. Scatter a few smoked almonds over the salad to garnish, if using.

COOK'S TIP
For extra colour, add some cherry tomatoes and some thin strips of red and yellow peppers and garnish with a little grated carrot.

This is a Parragon Book
This edition published in 2003

Parragon
Queen Street House
4 Queen Street
Bath BA1 1HE, UK

Copyright © Parragon 2001

ISBN: 1-40540-102-8

Printed in China

NOTE

This book uses metric and imperial measurements. Follow the same units
of measurement throughout; do not mix metric and imperial.
All spoon measurements are level: teaspoons are assumed to be 5 ml, and
tablespoons are assumed to be 15 ml. Unless otherwise stated,
milk is assumed to be full fat, eggs and individual vegetables such as potatoes
are medium, and pepper is freshly ground black pepper.

The nutritional information provided for each recipe is per serving or per person.
Optional ingredients variations or serving suggestions have
not been included in the calculations. The times given for each recipe are an approximate
guide only because the preparation times may differ according to the techniques used by
different people and the cooking times may vary as a result of the type of oven used.

Recipes using raw or very lightly cooked eggs should be
avoided by infants, the elderly, pregnant women, convalescents,
and anyone suffering from an illness.

The publisher would like to thank
Steamer Trading Cookshop, Lewes, East Sussex, for the kind loan of props.